MICROSOFT® OFFICE 97 FOR WINDOWS® FOR DUMMIES®

Quick Reference

MICROSOFT®
OFFICE 97
FOR WINDOWS® FOR
DUMMIES®

Quick Reference

by Doug Lowe

IDG Books Worldwide, Inc.
An International Data Group Company

Foster City, CA ✦ Chicago, IL ✦ Indianapolis, IN ✦ Southlake, TX

Microsoft® Office 97 For Windows® For Dummies® Quick Reference

Published by
IDG Books Worldwide, Inc.
An International Data Group Company
919 E. Hillsdale Blvd.
Suite 400
Foster City, CA 94404
www.idgbooks.com (IDG Books Worldwide Web site)
www.dummies.com (Dummies Press Web site)

Library of Congress Catalog Card No.: 96-79261

ISBN: 0-7645-0062-7

Printed in the United States of America

10 9 8 7 6 5 4

1P/SW/RR/ZX/IN

Distributed in the United States by IDG Books Worldwide, Inc.

Distributed by Macmillan Canada for Canada; by Transworld Publishers Limited in the United Kingdom; by IDG Norge Books for Norway; by IDG Sweden Books for Sweden; by Woodslane Pty. Ltd. for Australia; by Woodslane Enterprises Ltd. for New Zealand; by Longman Singapore Publishers Ltd. for Singapore, Malaysia, Thailand, and Indonesia; by Simron Pty. Ltd. for South Africa; by Toppan Company Ltd. for Japan; by Distribuidora Cuspide for Argentina; by Livraria Cultura for Brazil; by Ediciencia S.A. for Ecuador; by Addison-Wesley Publishing Company for Korea; by Ediciones ZETA S.C.R. Ltda. for Peru; by WS Computer Publishing Corporation, Inc., for the Philippines; by Unalis Corporation for Taiwan; by Contemporanea de Ediciones for Venezuela; by Computer Book & Magazine Store for Puerto Rico; by Express Computer Distributors for the Caribbean and West Indies. Authorized Sales Agent: Anthony Rudkin Associates for the Middle East and North Africa.

For general information on IDG Books Worldwide's books in the U.S., please call our Consumer Customer Service department at 800-762-2974. For reseller information, including discounts and premium sales, please call our Reseller Customer Service department at 800-434-3422.

For information on where to purchase IDG Books Worldwide's books outside the U.S., please contact our International Sales department at 415-655-3200 or fax 415-655-3295.

For information on foreign language translations, please contact our Foreign & Subsidiary Rights department at 415-655-3021 or fax 415-655-3281.

For sales inquiries and special prices for bulk quantities, please contact our Sales department at 415-655-3200 or write to the address above.

For information on using IDG Books Worldwide's books in the classroom or for ordering examination copies, please contact our Educational Sales department at 800-434-2086 or fax 817-251-8174.

For press review copies, author interviews, or other publicity information, please contact our Public Relations department at 415-655-3000 or fax 415-655-3299.

For authorization to photocopy items for corporate, personal, or educational use, please contact Copyright Clearance Center, 222 Rosewood Drive, Danvers, MA 01923, or fax 508-750-4470.

About the Author

Doug Lowe has written more than 30 computer books, including IDG Books Worldwide's *PowerPoint 97 For Windows For Dummies, Word 97 SECRETS,* and *Internet Explorer 3.0 For Dummies,* and he knows how to present boring technostuff in a style that is both entertaining and enlightening. He lives in sunny Fresno, California, with his wife Debbie, three adorable daughters, and two female golden retrievers, and he considers himself significantly outnumbered.

ABOUT IDG BOOKS WORLDWIDE

Welcome to the world of IDG Books Worldwide.

IDG Books Worldwide, Inc., is a subsidiary of International Data Group, the world's largest publisher of computer-related information and the leading global provider of information services on information technology. IDG was founded more than 25 years ago and now employs more than 8,500 people worldwide. IDG publishes more than 275 computer publications in over 75 countries (see listing below). More than 60 million people read one or more IDG publications each month.

Launched in 1990, IDG Books Worldwide is today the #1 publisher of best-selling computer books in the United States. We are proud to have received eight awards from the Computer Press Association in recognition of editorial excellence and three from *Computer Currents'* First Annual Readers' Choice Awards. Our best-selling *...For Dummies®* series has more than 30 million copies in print with translations in 30 languages. IDG Books Worldwide, through a joint venture with IDG's Hi-Tech Beijing, became the first U.S. publisher to publish a computer book in the People's Republic of China. In record time, IDG Books Worldwide has become the first choice for millions of readers around the world who want to learn how to better manage their businesses.

Our mission is simple: Every one of our books is designed to bring extra value and skill-building instructions to the reader. Our books are written by experts who understand and care about our readers. The knowledge base of our editorial staff comes from years of experience in publishing, education, and journalism — experience we use to produce books for the '90s. In short, we care about books, so we attract the best people. We devote special attention to details such as audience, interior design, use of icons, and illustrations. And because we use an efficient process of authoring, editing, and desktop publishing our books electronically, we can spend more time ensuring superior content and spend less time on the technicalities of making books.

You can count on our commitment to deliver high-quality books at competitive prices on topics you want to read about. At IDG Books Worldwide, we continue in the IDG tradition of delivering quality for more than 25 years. You'll find no better book on a subject than one from IDG Books Worldwide.

IDG BOOKS
WORLDWIDE

John Kilcullen
CEO
IDG Books Worldwide, Inc.

Steven Berkowitz
President and Publisher
IDG Books Worldwide, Inc.

Eighth Annual Computer Press Awards ≥1992

Ninth Annual Computer Press Awards ≥1993

Tenth Annual Computer Press Awards ≥1994

Eleventh Annual Computer Press Awards ≥1995

IDG Books Worldwide, Inc., is a subsidiary of International Data Group, the world's largest publisher of computer-related information and the leading global provider of information services on information technology. International Data Group publishes over 275 computer publications in over 75 countries. Sixty million people read one or more International Data Group publications each month. International Data Group's publications include: **ARGENTINA:** Buyer's Guide, Computerworld Argentina, PC World Argentina; **AUSTRALIA:** Australian Macworld, Australian PC World, Australian Reseller News, Computerworld, IT Casebook, Network World, Publish, Webmaster; **AUSTRIA:** Computerwelt Osterreich, Networks Austria, PC Tip Austria; **BANGLADESH:** PC World Bangladesh; **BELARUS:** PC World Belarus; **BELGIUM:** Data News; **BRAZIL:** Annuário de Informática, Computerworld, Connections, Macworld, PC Player, PC World, Publish, Reseller News, Supergamepower; **BULGARIA:** Computerworld Bulgaria, Network World Bulgaria, PC & MacWorld Bulgaria; **CANADA:** CIO Canada, Client/Server World, ComputerWorld Canada, InfoWorld Canada, NetworkWorld Canada, WebWorld; **CHILE:** Computerworld Chile, PC World Chile; **COLOMBIA:** Computerworld Colombia, PC World Colombia; **COSTA RICA:** PC World Centro America; **THE CZECH AND SLOVAK REPUBLICS:** Computerworld Czechoslovakia, Macworld Czech Republic, PC World Czechoslovakia; **DENMARK:** Communications World Danmark, Computerworld Danmark, Macworld Danmark, PC World Danmark, Techworld Denmark; **DOMINICAN REPUBLIC:** PC World Republica Dominicana; **ECUADOR:** PC World Ecuador; **EGYPT:** Computerworld Middle East, PC World Middle East; **EL SALVADOR:** PC World Centro America; **FINLAND:** MikroPC, Tietoverkko, Tietoviikko; **FRANCE:** Distributique, Hebdo, Info PC, Le Monde Informatique, Macworld, Reseaux & Telecoms, WebMaster France; **GERMANY:** Computer Partner, Computerwoche, Computerwoche Extra, Computerwoche FOCUS, Global Online, Macwelt, PC Welt; **GREECE:** Amiga Computing, GamePro Greece, Multimedia World; **GUATEMALA:** PC World Centro America; **HONDURAS:** PC World Centro America; **HONG KONG:** Computerworld Hong Kong, PC World Hong Kong, Publish in Asia; **HUNGARY:** ABCD CD-ROM, Computerworld Szamitastechnika, Internetto online Magazine, PC World Hungary, PC-X Magazin Hungary; **ICELAND:** Tolvuheimur PC World Island; **INDIA:** Information Communications World, Information Systems Computerworld, PC World India, Publish in Asia; **INDONESIA:** InfoKomputer PC World, Komputek Computerworld, Publish in Asia; **IRELAND:** ComputerScope, PC Live!; **ISRAEL:** Macworld Israel, People & Computers/Computerworld; **ITALY:** Computerworld Italia, Macworld Italia, Networking Italia, PC World Italia; **JAPAN:** DTP World, Macworld Japan, Nikkei Personal Computing, OS/2 World Japan, SunWorld Japan, Windows NT World, Windows World Japan; **KENYA:** PC World East African; **KOREA:** Hi-Tech Information, Macworld Korea, PC World Korea; **MACEDONIA:** PC World Macedonia; **MALAYSIA:** Computerworld Malaysia, PC World Malaysia, Publish in Asia; **MALTA:** PC World Malta; **MEXICO:** Computerworld Mexico, PC World Mexico; **MYANMAR:** PC World Myanmar; **NETHERLANDS:** Computer! Totaal, LAN Internetworking Magazine, LAN World Buyers Guide, Macworld Netherlands, Net, WebWereld; **NEW ZEALAND:** Absolute Beginners Guide and Plain & Simple Series, Computer Buyer, Computer Industry Directory, Computerworld New Zealand, MTB, Network World, PC World New Zealand; **NICARAGUA:** PC World Centro America; **NORWAY:** Computerworld Norge, CW Rapport, Datamagasinet, Financial Rapport, Kursguide Norge, Macworld Norge, Multimediaworld Norge, PC World Ekspress Norge, PC World Nettverk, PC World Norge, PC World ProduktGuide Norge; **PAKISTAN:** Computerworld Pakistan; **PANAMA:** PC World Panama; **PEOPLE'S REPUBLIC OF CHINA:** China Computer Users, China Computerworld, China InfoWorld, China Telecom World Weekly, Computer & Communication, Electronic Design China, Electronics Today, Electronics Weekly, Game Software, PC World China, Popular Computer Week, Software Weekly, Software World, Telecom World; **PERU:** Computerworld Peru, PC World Profesional Peru, PC World SoHo Peru; **PHILIPPINES:** Click!, Computerworld Philippines, PC World Philippines, Publish in Asia; **POLAND:** Computerworld Poland, Computerworld Special Report Poland, Cyber, Macworld Poland, Networld Poland, PC World Komputer; **PORTUGAL:** Cerebro/PC World, Computerworld/Correio Informático, Dealer World Portugal, Mac*In/PC*In Portugal, Multimedia World; **PUERTO RICO:** PC World Puerto Rico; **ROMANIA:** Computerworld Romania, PC World Romania, Telecom Romania, Telecom Romania; **RUSSIA:** Computerworld Russia, Mir PK, Publish, Seti; **SINGAPORE:** Computerworld Singapore, PC World Singapore, Publish in Asia; **SLOVENIA:** Monitor; **SOUTH AFRICA:** Computing SA, Network World SA, Software World SA; **SPAIN:** Communications World España, Computerworld España, Dealer World España, Macworld España, PC World España; **SRI LANKA:** Infolink PC World; **SWEDEN:** CAP&Design, Computer Sweden, Corporate Computing Sweden, Internetworld Sweden, it.branschen, Macworld Sweden, MaxiData Sweden, MikroDatorn, Nätverk & Kommunikation, PC World Sweden, PCaktiv, Windows World Sweden; **SWITZERLAND:** Computerworld Schweiz, Macworld Schweiz, PCtip; **TAIWAN:** Computerworld Taiwan, Macworld Taiwan, NEW ViSiON/Publish, PC World Taiwan, Windows World Taiwan; **THAILAND:** Publish in Asia, Thai Computerworld; **TURKEY:** Computerworld Turkiye, Macworld Turkiye, Network World Turkiye, PC World Turkiye; **UKRAINE:** Computerworld Kiev, Multimedia World Ukraine, PC World Ukraine; **UNITED KINGDOM:** Acorn User UK, Amiga Action UK, Amiga Computing UK, Apple Talk UK, Computing, Macworld, Parents and Computers UK, PC Advisor, PC Home, PSX Pro, The WEB; **UNITED STATES:** Cable in the Classroom, CIO Magazine, Computerworld, DOS World, Federal Computer Week, GamePro Magazine, InfoWorld, I-Way, Macworld, Network World, PC Games, PC World, Publish, Video Event, THE WEB Magazine, and WebMaster; online webzines: JavaWorld, NetscapeWorld, and SunWorld Online; **URUGUAY:** InfoWorld Uruguay; **VENEZUELA:** Computerworld Venezuela, PC World Venezuela, and PC World Vietnam. 3/24/97

Acknowledgments

Thanks to Mary Goodwin for keeping this book on track in spite of hectic schedules. And to William A. Barton and Jim McCarter: Thanks for your editorial and technical contributions in making this book both readable and accurate.

Publisher's Acknowledgments

We're proud of this book; please register your comments through our IDG Books Worldwide Online Registration Form located at http://my2cents.dummies.com.

Some of the people who helped bring this book to market include the following:

Acquisitions, Development, and Editorial

Project Editor: Mary Goodwin

Acquisitions Editor: Gareth Hancock

Product Development Director: Mary Bednarek

Copy Editor: William A. Barton

Technical Editor: Jim McCarter

Editorial Manager: Seta K. Frantz

Editorial Assistant: Chris H. Collins

Production

Project Coordinator: Regina Snyder

Layout and Graphics: E. Shawn Aylsworth, Linda M. Boyer, J. Tyler Connor, Dominique DeFelice, Maridee V. Ennis, Angela F. Hunckler, Todd Klemme, Jane E. Martin, Drew R. Moore, Elizabeth Cárdenas-Nelson, Laura Puranen, Anna Rohrer, Brent Savage

Proofreaders: Sandra Profant, Joel K. Draper, Nancy Price, Robert Springer, Karen York

Indexer: Sharon Duffy

General and Administrative

IDG Books Worldwide, Inc.: John Kilcullen, CEO; Steven Berkowitz, President and Publisher

IDG Books Technology Publishing: Brenda McLaughlin, Senior Vice President and Group Publisher

Dummies Technology Press and Dummies Editorial: Diane Graves Steele, Vice President and Associate Publisher; Mary Bednarek, Acquisitions and Product Development Director; Kristin A. Cocks, Editorial Director

Dummies Trade Press: Kathleen A. Welton, Vice President and Publisher; Kevin Thornton, Acquisitions Manager; Maureen F. Kelly, Editorial Coordinator

IDG Books Production for Dummies Press: Beth Jenkins, Production Director; Cindy L. Phipps, Manager of Project Coordination, Production Proofreading, and Indexing; Kathie S. Schutte, Supervisor of Page Layout; Shelley Lea, Supervisor of Graphics and Design; Debbie J. Gates, Production Systems Specialist; Robert Springer, Supervisor of Proofreading; Debbie Stailey, Special Projects Coordinator; Tony Augsburger, Supervisor of Reprints and Bluelines; Leslie Popplewell, Media Archive Coordinator

Dummies Packaging and Book Design: Patti Crane, Packaging Specialist; Lance Kayser, Packaging Assistant; Kavish + Kavish, Cover Design

◆

The publisher would like to give special thanks to Patrick J. McGovern, without whom this book would not have been possible.

◆

Contents at a Glance

Table of Contents

How to Use This Book

Greetings! Welcome to *Microsoft Office 97 For Windows For Dummies Quick Reference,* the Microsoft Office 97 reference book that is recommended by 3 out of 4 computer gurus surveyed.

You have found the perfect book if you are one of the hapless souls who must use Microsoft Office 97 but don't really want to become an expert in anything remotely related to computers. This book is a guiding star for those of you who still have a life outside of Office 97 and don't want to spend hours figuring out how to do things that should be easy.

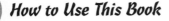

About This Book

This book does not teach you how to use Microsoft Office 97 from the ground up. If you're a complete beginner when it comes to Office 97, I suggest that you pick up a copy of Wally Wang and Roger Parker's *Microsoft Office 97 For Windows For Dummies*. Or take a shopping cart through the computer book aisle at your local bookstore and get copies of *Word 97 For Windows For Dummies* (Dan Gookin), *Excel 97 For Windows For Dummies* (Greg Harvey), *PowerPoint 97 For Windows For Dummies* (Yours Truly), *Microsoft Outlook For Dummies* (Bill Dyszel), and *Access 97 For Windows For Dummies* (John Kaufeld), all from IDG Books Worldwide, Inc. These books tell you everything you need to know about using the programs that come with Office 97.

This book is meant to be more of an "I forgot how to do that" book. It's for those embarrassing moments when you should know how to insert a chart, but you can't quite remember which command to use. Or when you want to quickly look up the keyboard shortcut that enables you to switch to Outline view. Or when you know that there's a quick way to do a Word 97 mail merge using data stored in an Access 97 database, but you're not quite sure what it is.

Turn to this book when you want 30-Second-Right-Now-Don't-Waste-My-Time answers to your questions. You don't find pages and pages of tireless prose exploring all the subtle nuances of each Office 97 command. Instead, you get concise explanations of how to perform what I think are the most important and useful tasks and procedures.

How to Use This Book

Keep this book within arm's reach of your computer. Whenever you're about to do something you're not 100-percent sure about, grab this book before reaching for your mouse and look up what you're about to do to refresh your memory.

The best way to use this book is probably to use the index to find the procedure you're having trouble with and then turn to the indicated page to find out how to perform the procedure. Tasks that are common to all the programs — such as opening and closing files — are found in Part I. Procedures for using the various programs together are found in Part IX. Tasks that are specific to the individual programs are found in the parts in between.

What Are All These Parts?

This book is divided into the following nine parts:

Part I: Getting to Know Microsoft Office 97. This brief introduction to Microsoft Office 97 explains what each Office 97 program does. It also describes the little mini-applications that come with Office 97, such as WordArt and Organization Chart.

Part II: Doing Common Chores. This part describes several features common to all the programs, such as opening and closing files, working with the Office Assistant, and so on.

Part III: Word 97. This part contains reference information about Word 97 for Windows, the ultimate word processing program. The part also summarizes the steps for common procedures that you perform in Word 97.

Part IV: Excel 97. This part covers Excel 97, the last word in spreadsheet programs. You find information about the most common Excel 97 functions and procedures.

Part V: PowerPoint 97. This part covers PowerPoint 97, the desktop presentation program for creating slides, overhead transparencies, and on-screen slide shows. Once again, I provide information about the most common PowerPoint 97 procedures.

Part VI: Access 97. If you own the Professional Edition of Microsoft Office 97, you'll appreciate this part, which covers this top-notch database program.

Part VII: Outlook. Office 97 comes with a new program called Outlook, which not only enables you to keep an up-to-date appointment and address book on your computer, but also handles all your e-mail. This part covers the most common procedures for Outlook.

Part VIII: The Microsoft Office 97 Applets. Microsoft Office 97 comes with a number of smaller programs called *applets* that you can use from within the other Office 97 programs. These miniprograms include Graph, Equation Editor, WordArt, OrgChart, and ClipArt Gallery. Find out how to use them in this part.

Part IX: Working Together. This "Office 97 is greater than the sum of its parts" part shows you how to use the various Office 97 programs together by exchanging information between programs. For example, you discover how to perform a Word 97 mail merge with Excel 97 or Access 97 data, create a PowerPoint 97 presentation from a Word 97 outline, and analyze Access 97 data in Excel 97.

What All the Pretty Pictures Mean

Just before this book went to the printer, I pelted it with a semiauto-matic icon assault rifle, now illegal in 17 states. As a result, this book is strewn with little pictures designed to convey information quickly. Here's the lowdown on the icons you find in these pages:

 Danger! Danger! You may be putting your files, your system, or yourself at risk if you don't heed these warnings.

 This little tidbit of helpful information can save you time and effort.

 This icon points out the quickest way to do something.

 Watch it; something that's quirky or that doesn't work the way you think it should lurks near.

 This icon points to a neat feature of Office 97 and the programs that come with it or perhaps a helpful shortcut or insider tip.

This icon points out ways to use Microsoft's new IntelliMouse, which has that funky wheel-thing going on between the mouse buttons.

This icon indicates that you can find more information about a particular topic in *Microsoft Office 97 For Windows For Dummies* or one of the other *...For Dummies* books.

Other Stuff You Should Know

On occasion, this book directs you to use specific keyboard shortcuts to get things done. Suppose that you see something such as the following:

Ctrl+Z

It means to press and hold the Ctrl key as you press the Z key and then to release both keys together. You don't actually type the plus sign.

Sometimes I tell you to use a menu command, as follows:

File⇨Open

This line means to use the keyboard or mouse to open the File menu and then choose the Open command. The underlined letters are the keyboard hot keys for the command. You can use the hot keys first by pressing the Alt key. In the preceding example, you could press and release the Alt key, press and release the F key, and then press and release the O key.

Anything that I instruct you to type appears in bold, as follows:

Type **b:setup** in the Run dialog box.

Type the boldfaced text exactly as it appears; spaces between words *are* important.

Part 1

Getting to Know Microsoft Office 97

One thing's for sure: You get your money's worth with Microsoft Office 97. In one convenient bundle, you get a world-class word processor, spreadsheet, presentation program, and database program. Plus you get a grab bag full of other useful programs. What a bargain!

This part provides a general overview of the various pieces that make up Office 97 so that you can get an idea of how the pieces fit together.

In this part . . .

✔ **What each of the Office 97 applications does**

✔ **The difference between Office 97 and Office 97 Professional**

✔ **Shared Office 97 components**

Seeing What All Those Programs Do

The standard Microsoft Office 97 package comes with four programs: Word 97, Excel 97, PowerPoint 97, and Outlook. The more expensive Microsoft Office 97 Professional Edition comes with the same four programs plus a database program called Access 97.

Word 97

Microsoft Word 97 for Windows (also called Word 8) is one of the best word processing programs available. The program enables you to create documents of all shapes and sizes, from small letters and memos to medium-sized term papers and reports to humongous books and health care reform proposals.

Besides word processing, Word 97 offers many interesting features. Here are just a few of the brand-spanking new features of Word 97:

+ A new Web publishing feature enables you to create HTML documents that you can publish on the World Wide Web.

+ A new drawing feature enables you to create three-dimensional shapes and create text frames in which text flows from one frame to the next.

+ A new feature called AutoComplete attempts to guess at what you intend to type before you even finish typing a word.

See Part III of this book for more information about Word 97.

Excel 97

Excel 97, a spreadsheet program, is the bean-counter of the Office 97 operation. Excel 97 excels at adding up budget totals, calculating sales commissions, figuring loan payments, and performing other math-oriented chores. As do other spreadsheet programs, Excel 97 presents its data as a large table that consists of rows and columns. The intersection of a row and column is called a *cell*. You can use cells to store text, numbers, or formulas that calculate results based on the contents of other cells.

Office 97 comes with Version 8 of Excel, which is often called Excel 97. For Version 8, Microsoft has added several useful new features, including new Internet-related capabilities that enable you to create links to information on the World Wide Web and new Wizards that simplify several complicated spreadsheet tasks.

You find reference information for Excel 97 in Part IV of this book.

PowerPoint 97

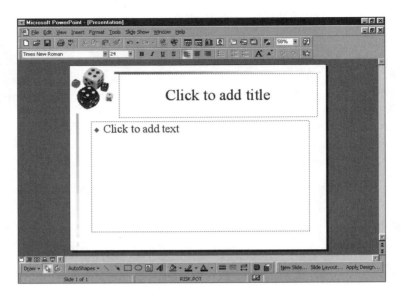

PowerPoint 97 (also sometimes known as PowerPoint 8) is the oddball program of the Office 97 suite. Many people buy Office 97 because they need a word processor and a spreadsheet program, and buying the standard Office 97 package is cheaper than buying Word 97 and Excel 97 separately. So the rest of what comes with Office 97 is basically free. And that includes PowerPoint 97.

So what the heck is PowerPoint 97? It is a desktop presentation program, which means that the program is designed to help you make presentations. You can use PowerPoint 97 whether you're speaking in front of hundreds of people at a shareholders' meeting, to a group of sales reps at a sales conference, or with a client one-on-one at a restaurant.

If you work with overhead transparencies or 35mm slides, PowerPoint 97 is just the program you need. PowerPoint 97 can create slides in any of several formats and can also create handouts for your audience as well as notes for you so that you don't get lost in the middle of your speech.

You can also use PowerPoint 97 to create HTML files that you can publish on the World Wide Web.

Check out Part V of this book for reference information about PowerPoint 97.

Access 97

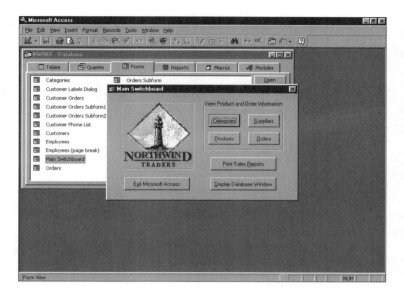

Access 97, a database program, is the computer equivalent of the shoe box in which you store your tax records. Access 97 is better than the shoe box in many ways, because Access keeps your records in order, enables you to print reports that list and summarize your data in any form imaginable, and doesn't crumple your papers. On the negative side, Access 97 is a lot harder to use than your average shoe box.

Access 97 (also known as Access Version 8) comes with the more expensive Microsoft Office 97 Professional; the program isn't in the bargain-basement, standard Office 97 package.

Of the programs that come with Office 97, Access 97 is the hardest one to conquer. Database programs such as Access 97 are well-suited for keeping mailing lists, but if a mailing list is the only reason you need Access 97, don't bother. Word 97 does a pretty good job of storing mailing lists all by itself.

You can also use Access 97 to set up databases that you can access from the Internet's World Wide Web.

See Part VI of this book for more information about Access 97.

Outlook

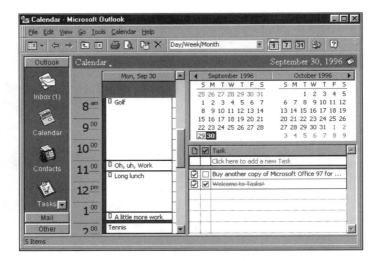

Outlook is a brand-new member of the Office 97 family, replacing the older and more-limited Schedule+. Outlook is the computer equivalent of one of those fancy combination appointment book/address books — a time-management program that enables you to schedule appointments, create a To Do list, and keep track of your important contacts. But more than that, Outlook is also an all-in-one e-mail program from which you can send and receive electronic mail over the Internet, your office network, or any of several popular online services.

See Part VII of this book for more information about Outlook.

Looking at Those Little Applet Programs

In addition to the programs just described, Office 97 comes with a number of smaller programs that work alongside — and in some cases from within — the other Office 97 programs. These smaller programs are often called *applets* and include Binder, Clip Gallery, Equation Editor, Graph, OrgChart, WordArt, and Photo Editor.

In many cases, the applet programs are so closely tied to Word 97, Excel 97, PowerPoint 97, or Access 97 that distinguishing the applet as a separate program is hard. The best examples of this are Graph and WordArt. In other cases, such as Organization Chart and Clip Gallery, the applet programs are separate programs but run from within Word 97, Excel 97, PowerPoint 97, or Access 97. Still others are stand-alone programs that run separately from the main Office 97 programs.

Reference information for the applet programs is located in Part VIII of this book.

Binder

Binder enables you to create *binders,* which you can think of as "super documents" that contain individual documents created by other Office 97 programs. You use binders to bring together different types of related documents. Binder is one of the stand-alone programs that doesn't run from within the main Office 97 programs.

Clip Gallery

Clip Gallery is a centralized storehouse for multimedia clips, including clip art, pictures, sounds, and videos. Clip Gallery eliminates riffling through various directories trying to find just the right bit of clip art based on an esoteric DOS filename. What's more, Clip Gallery enables you to connect to the Internet to access a special Internet site Microsoft created to download additional multimedia goodies.

Clip Gallery is a separate program that you must run from within one of the main Office 97 programs.

Equation Editor

Move over, Einstein! Office 97 comes with an equation editor called — hold on to your hat — Microsoft Equation Editor, which can help you draw simple equations such as e=mc² or complex equations such as the following:

$$t = \frac{\overline{X}_A - \overline{X}_B}{\sqrt{\dfrac{(n_A - 1)s_A^2 + ((n_B - 1)s_B^2}{n_A + n_B - 2}} \sqrt{\dfrac{1}{n_A} + \dfrac{1}{n_B}}}$$

You can also access Equation Editor from Word 97, Excel 97, PowerPoint 97, or Access 97 by choosing Insert⇨Object.

Graph

Graph is the charting module that comes with Office 97. You can use Graph to create bar, line, and pie charts and a bevy of other chart types that come in handy from time to time. Graph is fully integrated with Word 97, Excel 97, PowerPoint 97, and Access 97, so it doesn't appear as a separate program even though, technically, it is.

Organization Chart

Organization Chart (sometimes called just OrgChart) enables you to make organizational charts that show who reports to whom and where the buck stops. You use OrgChart mostly from PowerPoint 97, but you can access the applet from the other Office 97 programs as well.

Organization Chart runs as a separate program in its own window. You can access it directly from a menu command in PowerPoint 97 or indirectly by choosing Insert⇨Object in any other Office 97 program.

WordArt

WordArt is a graphics program designed to create logos and other fancy text effects. You can use the applet to stretch text so that the text disappears into the horizon or follows a curve. You can also add a three-dimensional look to your words or otherwise embellish your text. WordArt can be accessed directly from a menu command or a toolbar button in Word 97, PowerPoint 97, or Excel 97.

Photo Editor

Microsoft Photo Editor is an imaging program that enables you to manipulate graphic images in various ways. For example, you can convert bland clip-art images into pictures that look as though the images were drawn with chalk and charcoal, pen and ink, or water colors — or even crafted in stained glass.

Photo Editor is a stand-alone program that does not run within any of the other Office 97 programs.

Part II

Doing Common Chores

This part presents procedures for certain basic tasks that work pretty much the same in all the Office 97 programs: opening and saving documents, printing, getting help, and so on.

In this part . . .

- Opening and closing documents
- Creating new documents and retrieving existing documents from disk
- Saving documents to disk
- Using Help
- Using the new mouse with the wheel thingy

Closing a File

To close a file, choose File➪Close or use the keyboard shortcut Ctrl+W.

 You don't need to close files before exiting a program. If you exit the program without closing a file, the program closes the file for you. But closing files with which you're no longer working is a good idea, because doing so saves memory, which may in turn help your programs run faster.

If you close a file and have made changes to the file since you last saved it, a dialog box appears, offering to save the changes for you. Click the Yes button to save the file before closing or click the No button to abandon any changes you made to the file.

 If you have only one file open and you close that file, you may discover that you've inadvertently rendered most of the program's commands inaccessible — they appear "grayed out" on the menus, and clicking them does nothing. Don't panic. Open another file or create a new file, and the commands return to life.

Creating a Document

You have several ways to create a new document in Word 97, Excel 97, or PowerPoint 97:

+ Choose File➪New. This command summons the New dialog box, which enables you to select which of several available templates you want to use as the basis of your new document. Word 97, Excel 97, and PowerPoint 97 all provide templates for the most common types of documents created in these programs.

+ Click the New button in the Standard toolbar, which bypasses the New dialog box and creates an empty new document.

+ Press Ctrl+N, which creates an empty new document as well.

For Access 97, the process of creating a new database is a bit more complicated and is covered in Part VI.

Exiting a Program

Had enough excitement for one day? Use any one of the following techniques to shut down your program:

+ Choose File➪Exit.

✦ Click the Close button that appears at the upper-right corner of the program window. The Close button is marked by an X, proving the old adage that X does indeed mark the spot.

✦ Press Alt+F4.

You can't abandon ship until you save your work. If you made changes to any files and haven't saved them, a dialog box asks whether you want to save your files. Tell it Yes.

Never, never, never, *never* ever just turn off your computer while a program is running. You may as well pour acid into the keyboard or run over the motherboard with a truck. Always exit all programs that are running *before* you turn off your computer. In fact, you should always notify Windows before you turn off your computer by clicking the Start button and then choosing the Sh<u>u</u>t Down command. This summons a Shut Down dialog box. To shut down your computer, click the <u>Y</u>es button.

Getting Help

Lost within the dark woods of Office 97 and don't know how to get out? Fret not, for all the Office 97 programs boast an excellent Help system that can answer all your questions — provided, of course, that you know what your questions are.

The following list summarizes the more notable methods of getting help:

✦ The universal Help key is F1. Press F1 at any time, and the Office Assistant rushes to your aid.

✦ If you press F1 while you're in the middle of something, the Office Assistant tries to figure out what you're doing and give you help tailored for that task. This slick little bit of wizardry is called *context-sensitive Help.*

✦ After you click <u>H</u>elp in the menu bar, you get an entire menu of Help stuff, most of which is only moderately helpful. Choosing <u>H</u>elp⇨<u>H</u>elp summons the Office Assistant. If you want to get the old-fashioned Windows-style help, choose <u>H</u>elp⇨<u>C</u>ontents and Index.

✦ You can also call up Help in just about any dialog box by clicking the question mark button that appears in the top-right corner of the dialog box. The mouse pointer changes to an arrow with a question mark grafted onto its back. You can then click anything in the dialog box to get specific information about that feature.

✦ You can also click the Office Assistant button on the Standard toolbar — the toolbar that sits just beneath the menu bar — to summon the Office Assistant.

✦ For a really cool kind of help, try choosing <u>H</u>elp➪What's <u>T</u>his? This Help feature changes the mouse pointer into a pointy question mark, with which you can click just about anything on-screen to get an explanation of the object you click.

Living with the Office Assistant

The Office Assistant is a friendly little helper that lives in its own little window. The Assistant watches you work and periodically chimes in with a tip about how you could perform a task more efficiently. And the Assistant is always there, either visible on-screen in its own little window or lurking behind the scene waiting for your summons.

If the Office Assistant is nowhere to be found, you can summon it quickly by clicking the Office Assistant button in the toolbar. To ask a question, click anywhere in the Office Assistant's window. A balloon dialog box appears, as shown in the following example:

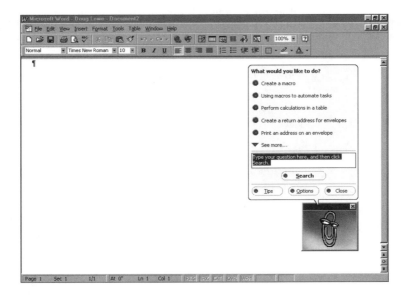

Tell the Assistant what you want to do by typing a few keywords in the balloon's text box (for example, you could type **create a bullet list**) and then click the Search button. The Assistant thinks for a moment and then shows you a list of Help topics that relate to your question. Click the topic you're interested in to display the Help.

If you don't like the little paper-clip Office Assistant that appears by default, you can change it to one of nine different Assistants: a cute little puppy, a funny cat made from folded paper, Shakespeare, Einstein, a Smiley Face, or several other choices. To change the Assistant's character, click the Office Assistant window to open the balloon dialog box and then click the Options button. The Office Assistant dialog box appears. Click the Gallery tab and then use the Back and Next buttons to choose the Assistant you want to use. Power Pup, as shown in the following figure, is my favorite.

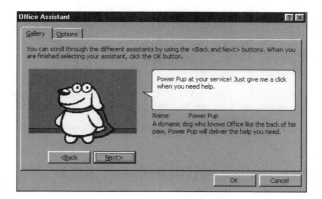

Click the OK button after you're done choosing your Assistant.

Help the old-fashioned way

When I was a kid, I didn't have fancy Office Assistants to bail me out if I needed help. No sir. I had to walk three miles through the snow in bare feet to get my help. That's why, in the Old Days, I appreciated all the help I could get.

If you yearn for the good old days, back when you actually had to *search* for Help topics, you can always revert to Windows-style Help. Here's how to search for Help on a specific topic the old-fashioned way:

1. Choose Help⇨Contents and Index.

The Help Topics dialog box appears, as shown here for Word 97.

2. Locate the topic for which you need information.

Browse through the Contents tab to find the help you're looking for. You can expand a Help topic by clicking a book icon, which reveals a list of more specific Help topics.

To search the Help index, click the Index tab. The index appears, as shown here:

Help Topics: Microsoft Word

Contents | Index | Find

1 Type the first few letters of the word you're looking for.

2 Click the index entry you want, and then click Display.

"hot spots"
"pitcher" doesn't tilt when I create linked text boxes
"pitcher" mouse pointer
  creating linked text boxes
"portable" documents
.cgm graphics files
.emf graphics files
.gif graphics files
.pct graphics files
  importing
.pcx files
  importing
.png files
  importing
\ instead of colon in index entries
\
  replaces colon in index entries

Display | Print... | Cancel

Type the word you want to look up in the text box labeled as option number 1. In the box labeled as option number 2, Help displays a list of the topics indexed under the word you type; from this list, click the topic you want to view and then click Display. Or just double-click the topic you want to view.

For a more thorough search, click the Find tab. The following dialog box appears:

Type the word you want to search for in the text box labeled as option number 1. Select one or more matching words from the first list box (labeled as number 2) to narrow the search and then click in the second list box (labeled as option number 3) the topic that you want to display; finally, click the Display button.

3. Click the Cancel button after you finish using Help.

Help on the Internet

You can also get help directly from Microsoft via the World Wide Web, assuming that you have access to the Internet from your computer. The Help menu includes a Microsoft on the Web command that features links to various Web sites that provide information about Microsoft Office products. Your best bet for online Help is to choose the Help➪Microsoft on the Web➪Online Support command. This command launches the Internet Explorer Web browser to display Microsoft's online support page for the program you're using. Here's what the support page looks like for Word 97:

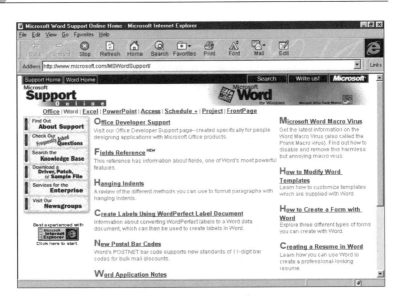

From this page, you can access useful articles about specific topics of interest. (For example, the previous figure includes links to articles about using fields, creating hanging indents, or working with bar codes.) Plus you can access a list of frequently asked questions or the Microsoft Knowledge Base, a huge searchable database that contains answers to thousands of technical questions.

But the most valuable link on the online support page is the Visit Our Newsgroups link. Click this link to enter Microsoft's product support newsgroups, where you can leave a detailed question that should be answered within a few days.

Note: The appearance of the online support page changes periodically, so it may not look exactly like the page shown in this section by the time you read this book. But the same basic information should still be available.

Shortcuts That Work Everywhere

The following tables list keyboard shortcuts and toolbar buttons that work in all (or at least most of) the Office 97 programs.

Editing Commands

Toolbar button	Keyboard Shortcut	Equivalent Command
✂	Ctrl+X	Edit⇨Cut
📋	Ctrl+C	Edit⇨Copy
📋	Ctrl+V	Edit⇨Paste
↶	Ctrl+Z	Edit⇨Undo
↷	Ctrl+Y	Edit⇨Redo
	Ctrl+A	Edit⇨Select All
	Ctrl+F	Edit⇨Find
	Ctrl+H	Edit⇨Replace

File Commands

Toolbar button	Keyboard Shortcut	Equivalent Command
🗋	Ctrl+N	File⇨New
📂	Ctrl+O or Ctrl+F12	File⇨Open
💾	Ctrl+S	File⇨Save
	F12	File⇨Save As
	Ctrl+W	File⇨Close
🖨	Ctrl+P	File⇨Print
	Alt+F4	File⇨Exit

Quick Formatting

Toolbar button	Keyboard Shortcut	Format Applied
B	Ctrl+B	Bold
I	Ctrl+I	Italic
U	Ctrl+U	Underline
	Ctrl+spacebar	Return to normal format

Switching Programs

Keyboard Shortcut	What It Does
Alt+Esc	Switches to the next program in line.
Alt+Tab	Displays the name of the next program in line. While holding the Alt key, press Tab to summon a list of icons for all the programs that are currently running. Keep pressing the Tab key until the icon for the program you want to switch to is highlighted and then release both keys to switch to that program.
Ctrl+Esc	Pops up the taskbar and the Start menu. Click the button on the taskbar for the program you want to switch to.

Macros

Macros enable you to record the commands you need to carry out common procedures. If you find yourself performing the same sequence of operations over and over again, you can often save a lot of time by recording these actions in a macro. Then, whenever you need to perform that repetitive task, all you need to do is click a button and the macro performs the task for you. The following procedures apply to Word 97, Excel 97, and PowerPoint 97. Access 97 supports macros, too, but Access 97 macros are a bit more complicated and aren't covered in this book. The other Office 97 programs (such as Outlook and Binder) do not support macros.

Word 97 and Excel 97 have long supported macros, but Office 97 is the first version in which macros are supported in PowerPoint 97. Moreover, for the programmer-types out there, Microsoft has finally consolidated the macro language that all the Office 97 applications use. Word 97, Excel 97, PowerPoint 97, and even Access 97 now all rely on Visual Basic for Applications (VBA), Microsoft's powerful programming language for creating application macros. Reference information on VBA itself can take up 200 pages (at the least), so I don't cover the subject in this book. For more information on Visual Basic, pick up a copy of *Visual Basic 4 For Windows For Dummies,* by Wallace Wang, published by IDG Books Worldwide, Inc.

Recording a macro

To record a macro, follow these steps:

1. Think about what you're going to do and rehearse the procedure to make sure that you *really* know what you're doing.

2. Choose Tools➪Macro➪Record New Macro to open the Record Macro dialog box.

This dialog box varies just slightly between Word 97, Excel 97, and PowerPoint 97. Here's how the Record Macro dialog box appears in Word 97:

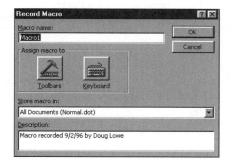

3. Type the name of your macro in the <u>M</u>acro name text box.

4. To make your macro accessible from a toolbar or the keyboard, click the <u>T</u>oolbars or <u>K</u>eyboard button, assign the shortcut, and then click the Close button.

To help you assign the keyboard shortcut, a dialog box appears with a text box in which you can type the shortcut. Type the shortcut key you want to use, click the <u>A</u>ssign button, and then click the Close button.

Note: The capability to assign the recorded macro to a keyboard shortcut while recording the macro is available *only* in Word 97. To assign a macro to a keyboard shortcut in PowerPoint 97 or Excel 97, choose Tools⇨Customize.

5. If you did not assign a keyboard shortcut in Step 4, click the OK button to begin recording the macro.

A little macro recorder toolbox appears, as shown here:

6. Type the keystrokes and menu commands that you want to record in the macro.

Click the Pause button in the macro toolbox if you need to temporarily suspend recording; click the Pause button again to resume recording.

7. After you finish recording, click the Stop button.

You can now run the macro by using the procedure described in the following section, "Running a macro." If the macro doesn't work, you may have made a mistake while recording it. Record the macro again.

To delete a macro that you recorded incorrectly, choose Tools⇨Macro⇨Macros to open the Macros dialog box. Select the macro you want to delete and then click the Delete button to delete it.

Running a macro

Follow this procedure to run a macro you previously recorded:

1. Choose Tools⇨Macro⇨Macros to access the Macro dialog box.

2. Select the macro you want to run from the list of macros currently available.

3. Click the Run button.

Note: If you assigned a keyboard shortcut or toolbar button to the macro, you can run the macro by pressing the assigned keyboard shortcut or clicking the macro's button.

Printing a File

Follow this procedure to print your masterpiece:

1. Make sure that your printer is turned on and ready to print.

2. Open the Print dialog box by choosing File⇨Print or pressing Ctrl+P.

The Print dialog box enables you to print a single page or range of pages and to print more than one copy of the document. It also enables you to change the paper size and orientation and to select the printer you want to use if more than one printer is available to your computer.

 To quickly print a single copy of your entire document without fussing with the Print dialog box, click the Print button in the Standard toolbar. One crisp copy of your document should appear on the printer.

Retrieving an Existing File

After you save your file to disk, you may want to retrieve the file later to make changes or to print it. You can find and open a file in at least the following four ways:

 ✦ Click the Open button in the Standard toolbar.

✦ Choose <u>F</u>ile⇨<u>O</u>pen.

✦ Press Ctrl+O.

✦ Press Ctrl+F12.

All four methods access the Open dialog box, which gives you a list of files from which to choose.

Open	? ✕
Look <u>i</u>n: 📁 My Documents ▾ 🔁 🗐 🖾 ⚏ ⚏ ⚏ ⚏ 🖾	
📄Letter to Bob Abbot.doc 📄Letter to my mom.doc 📄Sarah's Homework.doc	<u>O</u>pen Cancel A<u>d</u>vanced...
Find files that match these criteria:	
File <u>n</u>ame: ▾ Te<u>x</u>t or property: ▾	<u>F</u>ind Now
Files of <u>t</u>ype: Word Documents (*.doc) ▾ Last <u>m</u>odified: any time ▾	Ne<u>w</u> Search
3 file(s) found.	

Click the file you want and then click the <u>O</u>pen button or press Enter. If that file isn't listed as a choice, use the Look <u>i</u>n drop-down list to rummage about your disk until you find the file.

The fastest way to open a file from the Open dialog box is to double-click the name of the file you want to open. Doing so spares you from first clicking the filename and then clicking the <u>O</u>pen button.

Other controls on the Open dialog box are listed in the following table.

Control	What It Does
📁 My Documents ▾	Enables you to look in a different folder or drive.
🔁	Moves up one folder.
🗐	Displays your Favorites folder.
🗐	Adds the current folder or document to your Favorites folder.

All the Office 97 programs keep track of the last few files you opened and display the names of those files at the bottom of the <u>F</u>ile menu. To reopen a file that you opened recently, click the <u>F</u>ile menu and inspect the list of files at the bottom of the menu. If the filename you want appears in this list, click the filename to open that file.

Saving a File

After you finish your document, spreadsheet, or presentation, you can print that file and turn off your computer, right? Wrong! Your precious work is not safe until you *save* your work to a disk file. Turn off your computer before you save your work, and — poof! — your work vanishes as though David Copperfield were in town.

You can save a file to disk in the following four ways:

+ Click the Save button on the Standard toolbar.

+ Choose File➪Save.

+ Press Ctrl+S.

+ Press Shift+F12.

If you haven't yet saved the file to disk, the magical Save As dialog box appears, in which you can type the name you want to use for the file.

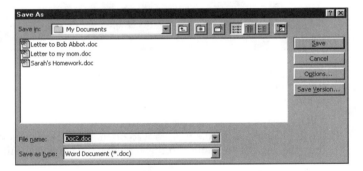

Type a filename for your file in the File name text box and then click the Save button to save the file. After you save the file, subsequent saves update the disk file with any changes you made to that file since you last saved the file.

Several interesting buttons and controls are available from the Save As dialog box:

Control	What It Does
My Documents ▼	Enables you to save the file in a different folder or drive.
🔼	Moves up one folder.
✳	Displays your Favorites folder.
📁	Creates a new folder.

Don't work on your file for hours at a time without saving. I found out the hard way to save my work — I lost six hours of work after the power went out once. Get into the habit of saving your work every few minutes, especially after making a significant change to a file.

Saving a File under a New Name

If you want to make a duplicate of the current file by saving the file under a different filename, follow these steps:

1. Choose File⇨Save As.

   The Save As dialog box appears. (See the preceding section, "Saving a File.")

2. Use the Save in drop-down list to rummage about until you find the drive and folder in which you want to save the file.

   Click the Create Folder button if you want to create a new folder instead of using an existing one.

3. Type a new name for the file in the File name text box.

4. Click the Save button.

Saving a File in HTML Format

HTML is a computer language that you use to format material for the Internet's World Wide Web. One of the hottest new features of Office 97 is that Word 97, Excel 97, PowerPoint 97, and Access 97 include a new Save as HTML command that converts your work to a format that you can display on the Web.

To save an Office document in HTML format, all you need to do is choose File⇨Save as HTML. What happens after you choose the command depends on which program you're using. In Word 97, a Save As dialog box appears and the entire document is converted to HTML. In Excel 97, PowerPoint 97, and Access 97, a Wizard appears, asking you to answer a few questions before converting your document to HTML.

 You can find more information about using the Save as HTML command in the parts devoted to each of the Office 97 programs.

Sending a File via E-Mail

 If your computer is connected to a network or to the Internet, you can send a copy of the file you're working on to a friend or co-worker via e-mail by following these steps:

1. Choose File⇨Send To⇨Mail Recipient.

A Message window similar to this one appears:

```
Categories.xls - Message                              _ □ X

File  Edit  View  Insert  Format  Tools  Compose  Help

Send  🖫 🖨  ✂ 🗐 🖺 🖉  📇 🔍  ▼  !  ↓  🗐 🖭

Arial        ▼  10  ▼  🔄  B  I  U  🗐 🗐 🗐 🗐 🖽 🖽

Message  | Options |

🛈 This message has not been sent.

To...  |                                             |
Cc...  |                                             |

Subject:  | Categories.xls                           |

        🖳
        Categories.xls
```

If the program asks you to specify a user profile, select the profile you normally use in sending and receiving e-mail. User profiles control such things as which e-mail services you have access to and where your address book is stored. If more than one person uses your computer, you can set up a separate profile for each user. If possible, talk the person responsible for setting up your company's e-mail system into configuring your user profile for you.

To...

2. Click the To... button to summon your address book, which should contain the e-mail addresses of the people you routinely correspond with.

3. Select the recipient from your address book and then click the OK button in the Address Book dialog box.

Send

4. Click the Send button to send the message.

Starting a Program

To start an Office 97 program, follow these steps:

1. Turn on your computer.

With luck, you need to flip only one switch to do so. But if your computer, monitor, and printer are plugged in separately, you must turn on each one separately. Windows 95 may take a moment to come to life; be patient.

2. Click the Start button.

   Normally, the Start button is located at the bottom left of the screen, but you can move it to any edge of the screen you want. If the Start button isn't visible anywhere on-screen, try moving the mouse all the way to the bottom edge of the screen to see whether the Start button appears. If that doesn't work, point to top, left, and right edges of the screen until the Start button appears.

   After you click the Start button, the Start menu pops up.

3. Point to Programs in the Start menu.

4. Locate and click the program you want to start from the menu that appears.

Switching among Programs

One of the best features of Windows 95 is that it enables you to run several programs at the same time and switch back and forth among those programs. By using this feature, for example, you can start up Word 97, PowerPoint 97, and Excel 97 at the same time and quickly switch to any of the three programs to access or exchange information among them.

After you have more than one program running, you can switch among them by using any of the following techniques:

+ **Press Alt+Esc:** You can switch to the next program in line by pressing Alt+Esc. If more than two programs are running, you may need to press this key combination several times to get to the program you want.

  You can reverse the order in which Windows switches to programs by pressing Alt+Shift+Esc instead.

+ **Press Alt+Tab:** Alt+Tab displays a menu of icons representing all of the programs currently running in a window that appears in the middle of the screen. To switch to a program, hold down the Alt key and press the Tab key repeatedly until you select the program you want to use. Then release both keys to switch to that program.

+ **Use the taskbar:** You can switch among programs easily by using the taskbar. Just click the button in the taskbar that represents the program to which you want to switch — and you're there!

The taskbar usually sits at the bottom of the screen, but you can also configure the taskbar to rest on any edge of the screens. You can even configure the taskbar so that the feature vanishes entirely if not in use. In that case, you must move the mouse pointer to the extreme bottom edge of the screen (or the left, right, or top edge, if you moved the taskbar) to access the feature again. If all else fails, you can locate the taskbar by pressing Ctrl+Esc, which reveals the taskbar no matter where it is. (Pressing Ctrl+Esc also opens the Start menu as if you had clicked the Start button.) After you locate the taskbar, you can then switch to any other running program by clicking that program's button on the taskbar.

Using the IntelliMouse

If you have Microsoft's new IntelliMouse, you can use its wheel control to scroll through your document. Just roll the wheel to scroll forward and back or click the wheel to switch to "pan" mode, which enables you to scroll through your document by dragging the mouse up or down. Click the wheel again to quit pan mode. You can also zoom in and out by pressing and holding the Ctrl key as you roll the wheel on the IntelliMouse.

Working with Older Versions

I have good news, and I have bad news. The good news is that Microsoft added a bunch of new features to Office 97 that make the programs easier to use. The bad news is that, to do so, Microsoft had to change the file format it uses to store Office 97 documents. Why should you care about that? Because it means that documents created with Office 97 programs are not compatible with earlier versions of Office programs.

Don't be alarmed: All Office 97 programs can easily open all of your old Office documents and automatically convert them to the new Office 97 format. But unfortunately, older versions of Office programs can't open your Office 97 documents. If you create a document with Office 97 and then give the document to a friend who is running an older version of the program, your buddy can't open the document. Beware of this limitation if you need to exchange documents with other Office users.

Part III

Word 97

Microsoft Office 97 comes with the latest and greatest version of Microsoft's premier word processing program, Microsoft Word 97. (Word 97 is also known as Word 8.) This part covers the basics of using Word 97. You can find lots more information about Word 97 in *Word 97 For Windows For Dummies,* by Dan Gookin, published by IDG Books Worldwide, Inc.

In this part . . .

- ✓ Formatting your text
- ✓ Working with tabs
- ✓ Using styles to simplify formatting chores
- ✓ Creating footnotes, an index, a table of authorities, and a table of contents
- ✓ Using the spell checker
- ✓ Discovering the most useful Word 97 keyboard shortcuts

Borders

To add a border around a text paragraph, follow these steps:

1. Place the insertion point anywhere in the paragraph to which you want to add a border.

2. Choose Format⇨Borders and Shading to access the Borders and Shading dialog box.

3. Select the type of border you want from the options in the Setting area of the dialog box's Borders tab (Box, Shadow, Three-D, or Custom, for example). Or click None if you want to remove the border.

4. Select a line style from the Style list, a color from the Color list, and a line width from the Width list if you don't like the default settings.

Scroll through the entire list of styles; Word 97 offers lots of interesting lines from which to choose. If you want each side of the border to have a different style, select the style and then click the appropriate button in the Preview area to apply the style to just that edge. After you change the style, the border around the mock paragraph in the Preview area changes so that you can see how your text appears with the border styles you selected.

5. Click the OK button or press Enter.

To get rid of a border, choose Format⇨Borders and Shading and then choose None for the border type.

Browsing

Word 97 offers a new Browse control located at the bottom of the scroll bar. Here's what it looks like:

After you click the Select Browse Object button sandwiched between the two double-arrow controls, a menu appears that enables you to access several navigation features from one convenient location, as shown in the following figure:

The first two buttons on this menu invoke the familiar Edit⇨Go to and Edit⇨Find commands. The ten remaining buttons change the unit by which the document is browsed after you click the double up or double down arrow controls immediately above and below the Select Browse Object button. The following table describes the function of each of the 12 buttons that appear on the Browse menu.

Button	*What It Does*
→	Invokes the Edit⇨Go to command.
🔍	Invokes the Edit⇨Find command.
✏	Browse by edits (works in conjunction with revision tracking).
☷	Browse by headings, as indicated by standard heading styles.
🖼	Browse by graphic objects.
▦	Browse by Word table objects.
{a}	Browse by Word fields.
🗐	Browse by endnote.
🗐	Browse by footnote.

(continued)

Button	What It Does
⬚	Browse by comments.
⬚	Browse by section.
⬚	Browse by page.

Bulleted Lists

To create a bulleted list, follow this procedure:

1. Type one or more paragraphs to which you want to add bullets.

2. Select the paragraphs to which you want to add bullets by dragging the mouse over them.

 3. Click the Bullets button on the Formatting toolbar.

To add additional items to the bulleted list, position the cursor at the end of one of the bulleted paragraphs and press Enter. Because the bullet is part of the paragraph format, the bullet format carries over to the new paragraph.

The Bullets button works like a toggle: Click the button once to add bullets and click the button again to remove them. To remove bullets from an entire list, select all the paragraphs in the list and click the Bullets button.

TIP

If you want to create a bulleted list as you compose your text, start by formatting the first paragraph with a bullet; Word 97 carries the bullet format over to subsequent paragraphs as you type them. After you finish typing your last bulleted paragraph, press Enter and then click the Bullets button again to "turn off" the bullet format.

To change the appearance of the bullet, choose Format⇨Bullets and Numbering and click the Bulleted tab. If the bullet style you want appears in the Bullets and Numbering dialog box, click that style and then click the OK button. Otherwise, click the Customize button to summon the Customize Bulleted List dialog box, click Bullet, and then select whichever oddball bullet character makes you happy.

Columns

To create multiple columns in your Word 97 document, follow these steps:

1. Click the Columns button on the Standard toolbar to open the drop-down menu, as shown in the following figure:

2. Drag the mouse to pick the number of columns you want. For example, if you want three columns in your document, drag the mouse over the columns until three are highlighted.

3. Release the mouse.

Voilá! The document appears formatted with the number of columns you select.

In normal view (choose View➪Normal), the text is formatted according to the width of the column, but the columns don't appear on-screen side by side. To see all columns side by side on-screen, switch to Page Layout view by choosing View➪Page Layout.

For a quick glimpse of how the columns appear after you print them, choose File➪Print Preview. After you have a good look, click the Close button to return to your document.

The Columns button enables you to set the number of columns, but the button doesn't enable you to control the size of each column or the amount of space between columns. To set the size of the columns and the space between them, choose Format➪Columns and play with its settings.

For more information, see Chapter 12 in *Word 97 For Windows For Dummies.*

Document Map

Word 97 includes a cool new feature called the *Document Map,* which enables you to view your document's outline side-by-side with the text, as shown here:

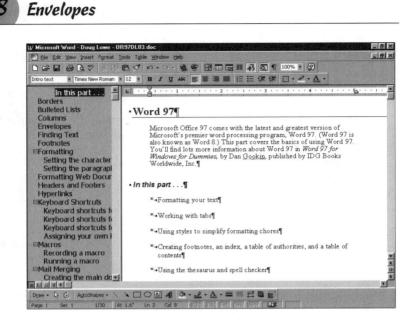

To show the Document Map, click the Document Map button found in the Standard toolbar. The Document Map button works like a toggle: Click it once to summon the Document Map; click it again to send the Document Map into exile.

After the Document Map is open, you can quickly move to any spot in your document simply by clicking the appropriate heading in the Document Map.

Envelopes

Choosing Tools➪Envelopes and Labels in Word 97 makes printing addresses on envelopes easy. Here's the blow-by-blow procedure:

1. If you're writing a letter to put in the envelope, create and print the letter first.

Doing so saves you the trouble of typing the mailing address twice.

2. Choose Tools➪Envelopes and Labels.

The Envelopes and Labels dialog box appears.

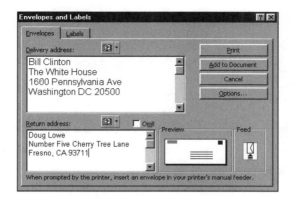

3. Check the address in the Delivery Address field.

Word 97 can usually automatically find the mailing address from an ordinary letter. If not, you must enter the address yourself.

If you want a return address printed on the envelope, type the return address in the space provided. (Notice that you can set a default return address by using the Tools⇨Options command, clicking the User Info tab, and typing your return address into the space provided there.)

4. Insert an envelope into your printer.

The Feed option in the Envelopes dialog box indicates how you should insert the envelope into the printer. If you want to feed the envelope differently, click the envelope icon in the Feed area of the Envelopes dialog box to open the Envelope Options dialog box. Select the feeding method you prefer and then click OK.

5. Click the Print button. That's all!

Finding Text

You can choose Edit⇨Find to find text anywhere in a document. Just follow these steps:

1. Choose Edit⇨Find or press Ctrl+F to open the Find and Replace dialog box.

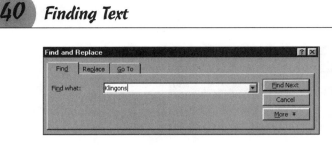

2. In the Fi_n_d What text box, type the text that you want to find.

You can type a single word or a phrase. Spaces are allowed.

3. Click the _F_ind Next button.

4. Wait a second while Word 97 searches your document.

After Word 97 finds the text, the program highlights the text on-screen. The Find dialog box remains on-screen so that you can click the _F_ind Next button to find yet another occurrence of the text. After Word 97 can find no more occurrences of the text, you see the following message in a separate dialog box:

```
Word has finished searching the document.
```

5. Click the OK button and get on with your life.

You can bail out of the Find and Replace dialog box by clicking the Cancel button or pressing Esc.

You can change how Word 97 searches for your text by clicking the _M_ore button in the Find and Replace dialog box to reveal a set of additional search options. The following options are available:

Search Option	What It Does
Search	Enables you to specify the direction in which Word 97 searches the document for text. The choices are Up, Down, and All. If you choose Up or Down, Word 97 stops at the beginning or end of the document and asks whether you want to continue the search. If you specify All, Word 97 automatically searches the entire document.
Match Case	Indicates that whether the text appears in uppercase or lowercase letters matters.
Find Whole Words Only	Finds your text only if the text appears as a whole word.
Find All Word Forms	Searches for all forms of the search text word. For example, if you search for *stink*, Word 97 also finds *stank* and *stunk*.

Search Option	What It Does
Use Wildcards	Enables you to include wildcard characters in the Find What text box. Here are three of the most useful wildcards:
?	Finds a single occurrence of any character. For example, **f?t** finds *fat* or *fit*.
*	Finds any combination of characters. For example, **b*t** finds any combination of characters that begins with *b* and ends with *t*, such as *bat*, *bait*, *ballast*, or *bacteriologist*.
[abc]	Finds any one of the characters enclosed in the brackets. For example, **b[ai]t** finds *bat* or *bit* but not *bet* or *but*.
Sounds Like	Finds text that is phonetically similar to the search text, even if the spelling varies.
Format	Enables you to search for text that has specific formatting applied — for example, to search for text formatted in the Arial font or with red type.
Special	Enables you to search for special characters such as as paragraph or tab marks.

Footnotes and Endnotes

Follow these steps to add footnotes or endnotes to your documents:

1. Place the cursor where you want the footnote reference number to appear in your text.

2. Choose Insert⇨Footnote to open the Footnote and Endnote dialog box.

3. If you want the note to appear at the bottom of the page, check the Footnote option. To create a note that appears at the end of the document, click the Endnote option.

Note: The first time you choose Insert⇨Footnote, the Footnote option is selected. Thereafter, the default setting is whatever you chose the last time you inserted a footnote or endnote. As a result, you need to worry about selecting Footnote or Endnote only if changing from footnotes to endnotes or back again.

4. Click the OK button.

A separate Footnotes or Endnotes window opens at the bottom of the screen, where you can type your footnote or endnote.

5. Click the Close button that appears in the Footnotes or Endnotes window after you finish typing in the footnote or endnote. The Footnotes or Endnotes window disappears.

Alternatively, you can just click back in the document to continue editing the document while leaving the Footnotes or Endnotes window open.

Word 97 automatically numbers footnotes for you and keeps the numbers in sequence as you insert and delete footnotes. Word 97 also automatically formats footnotes so that a footnote always appears at the bottom of the page in which the footnote is referenced, if possible. Long footnotes span several pages if necessary.

For an extra-quick way to create a footnote, press Ctrl+Alt+F.

To recall the Footnotes window, choose <u>V</u>iew⇨<u>F</u>ootnotes. You can then use the drop-down control that appears in the Footnotes window to display endnotes instead of footnotes.

If you goof up a footnote, double-click the footnote reference in the text. This opens the Footnote window and displays the footnote. You can then edit the note however you see fit.

To delete a footnote, select its footnote reference in the text and press Delete.

For more information about footnotes, see Chapter 11 of *Word 97 For Windows 95 For Dummies.*

Formatting

Word 97 gives you more ways to format your document than any mere mortal would ever need. The following sections present the more common formatting procedures.

Setting the character format

You can set character formats by using the formatting keyboard shortcuts or the buttons which appear in the Formatting toolbar, as described later in this part. Or you can use the following procedure to apply character formats via the F<u>o</u>rmat⇨<u>F</u>ont command:

1. Highlight the text to which you want to apply the formatting.

If you skip this step, Word 97 applies formatting to all new text you type until you repeat the procedure to deactivate the formatting.

2. Choose Format⇨Font.

The Font dialog box appears.

Font		? X
Font	Character Spacing	Animation

Font:
Times New Roman

𝕋 Stylus	
𝕋 Subway	
𝕋 Symbol	
𝕋 Tahoma	
𝕋 Times New Roman	

Font style:
Regular

Regular
Italic
Bold
Bold Italic

Size:
10

8
9
10
11
12

Underline:
(none)

Color:
Auto

Effects

☐ Strikethrough   ☐ Shadow   ☐ Small caps
☐ Double strikethrough   ☐ Outline   ☐ All caps
☐ Superscript   ☐ Emboss   ☐ Hidden
☐ Subscript   ☐ Engrave

Preview

Times New Roman

This is a TrueType font. This font will be used on both printer and screen.

Default...		OK	Cancel

3. Play with the controls in the Font dialog box to set the <u>F</u>ont, the Font st<u>y</u>le (bold, italic, and so on), and the <u>S</u>ize; select any of the Effects area check boxes you want (Stri<u>k</u>ethrough, Su<u>p</u>erscript, and so on); and use the drop-down list boxes to set the <u>U</u>nderline and <u>C</u>olor.

The Preview box at the bottom of the dialog box shows how text appears after Word 97 applies the formatting options you select.

4. Click the OK button after you have the character format just the way you want.

You can quickly set character formats by selecting the text to which you want the formats applied and then using one of the buttons on the Formatting toolbar or the keyboard shortcuts listed in the table in the section "Keyboard Shortcuts," later in this part. Alternatively, you can use the keyboard shortcut or click the button to enable the format, type some text, and then use the shortcut or button again to disable the format.

Setting the paragraph format

Follow these steps to apply paragraph formats by using the For-mat⇨Paragraph command:

1. Click anywhere in the paragraph you want to format. (You don't need to select the entire paragraph as long as the insertion point is somewhere in the paragraph you want to format.)

2. Choose Format⇨Paragraph.

The Paragraph dialog box appears.

Paragraph	? ×
Indents and Spacing	Line and Page Breaks

Alignment: Left ▼   Outline level: Body text ▼

Indentation
Left: 0" ⬍   Special: (none) ▼   By: ⬍
Right: 0" ⬍

Spacing
Before: 0 pt ⬍   Line spacing: Single ▼   At: ⬍
After: 0 pt ⬍

Preview

[Tabs...]   [OK]   [Cancel]

3. Play with the controls to set the paragraph's Alignment, Indentation, and Spacing. (You have lots of controls to play with, and you may not know which to choose. Fortunately, you can monitor the effect of each setting in the Preview box that appears in the Paragraph dialog box.)

4. Click the OK button after you finish formatting your paragraph.

You can quickly set paragraph formats by selecting the paragraphs you want to format and then using one of the buttons on the formatting toolbar or keyboard shortcuts listed in the table in the section "Keyboard Shortcuts," later in this part. To apply the format to a single paragraph, just place the insertion point anywhere in the paragraph.

Formatting Web Documents

Word 97 provides several additional formatting commands and options just for formatting HTML documents. (*HTML documents* are those that you can publish on the Internet's World Wide Web.) To create an HTML document rather than a normal Word 97 document, choose File➪New to open the New dialog box. Next, click the Web Pages tab and select the Blank Web Page template or the Web Page Wizard. (For more information about the Web Page Wizard, see the section "Using the Web Wizard," later in this part.)

You can use the following formatting commands while working with HTML documents:

◆ **Format➪Font:** Web documents have fewer font formatting options than do normal Word 97 documents. As a result, choosing Format➪Font accesses a special version of the standard Font dialog box that shows only those formatting options that work in HTML documents. This dialog box enables you to set the font, size, color, and style (bold, italic, underline, strikethrough, superscript, and subscript), as shown in the following figure:

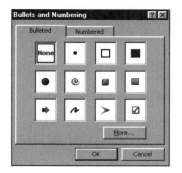

◆ **Format➪Bullets and Numbering:** The Bullets and Numbering command for Web pages is specially designed to enable you to use custom graphic bullets instead of standard, boring HTML bullets or to apply an HTML numbering style. Here is how this dialog box appears:

✦ **Format⇨Text Colors:** This command enables you to select the colors for body text, hyperlinks that no one has visited yet, and hyperlinks that someone has already visited.

✦ **Format⇨Scrolling Text:** Choose this command to create a marquee, in which text scrolls across the screen from one side to the other. Choosing this command displays the following dialog box:

Scrolling Text	✕

Scrolling Text Options | Size and Speed

Behavior: Scroll   Background Color: ☐ Auto

Direction: Left   Loop: Infinite

Type the Scrolling Text Here:

Sample Text

Preview:

Sample Text

OK   Cancel

You can play with the various settings in this dialog box to set the text that you want to scroll, the direction in which you want the text to scroll, and whether you want the text to scroll just once or to repeat in a loop. In addition, you can click the Size and Speed tab to set the size of the area within which the text scrolls and the speed at which the text scrolls.

✦ **Format⇨Background:** Use this command to set the color for the background of your Web page. You can also choose Format⇨Background⇨Fill Effects to create a textured background.

✦ **Insert⇨Horizontal Line:** This command opens a dialog box that enables you to select one of several different styles of horizontal lines to insert into your page, as shown in the following figure. Select a line style, click the style you want, and then click the OK button.

+ **Insert⇨Background Sound:** This command enables you to assign a sound that plays in the background whenever the Web page is on-screen.

+ **Insert⇨Forms:** This command enables you to insert Web form controls such as text boxes and command buttons on your Web pages.

+ **Insert⇨Hyperlink:** This command creates a link to another document. See the section "Hyperlinks," later in this part, for more information on hyperlinks.

Headers and Footers

To add a header or footer to a document, follow these steps:

1. Choose View⇨Header and Footer.

The Header and Footer toolbar appears, along with the header of the current page. (If you haven't yet created a header for the document, the header area is blank.)

> **Header and Footer**
>
> Insert AutoText ▾   Close

2. To switch between headers and footers, click the Header and Footer button in the toolbar.

3. Type your header or footer text in the header or footer area, formatting the text any way you want.

4. Click the other buttons in the Header and Footer toolbar to add the page numbers or the date or time. Here's what each button does:

Button	What It Does
🔢	Inserts the number of the current page.
🔢	Inserts the total number of pages in the document.
🔢	Enables you to specify a format for page numbers.
🔢	Inserts the date.
🕐	Inserts the time.

 5. Click the <u>C</u>lose button after you finish adding a header or footer.

 For more information, see Chapter 11 of *Word 97 For Windows For Dummies*.

Hyperlinks

A *hyperlink* is a bit of text or a graphic on a document that you can click to display another document. The hyperlink may lead to another location in the current document, another Office 97 document, or to a page on the Internet's World Wide Web.

To create a hyperlink in a Web document, follow these steps:

1. Select the text or graphic that you want to turn into a hyperlink.

2. Choose <u>I</u>nsert⇨Hyper<u>l</u>ink.

The Insert Hyperlink dialog box appears.

Insert Hyperlink ❓ ✖

<u>L</u>ink to file or URL:

[▼] [<u>B</u>rowse...]

Enter or locate the path to the document you want to link to. This can be an Internet address (URL), a document on your hard drive, or a document on your company's network.

Path: `<Link to containing document>`

<u>N</u>amed location in file: (Optional)

[   ] [Bro<u>w</u>se...]

If you want to jump to a specific location within the document, such as a bookmark, a named range, a database object, or a slide number, enter or locate that information above.

☑ <u>U</u>se relative path for hyperlink

[OK] [Cancel]

3. Type the Internet address (URL) in the Link to File or URL text box.

If you want to link to another document, just type the complete filename (for example, **somefile.doc** or **e:\docs\another.doc**). To link to a Web page at another site, type the complete URL of the page you want to link to (for example, http://www.somewhere.com/somepage.htm).

4. If you want to link to a specific location within a file, type the name of the location in the Named Location in File field.

The following table lists how named locations are created with Microsoft Office 97 applications.

Type of Document	How Named Locations Are Created
Word 97 document	Bookmarks (Insert⇨Bookmark)
Excel 97 worksheet	Range names (Insert⇨Name)
PowerPoint 97 presentation	Slide number
Access database	Any named database object

5. Click the OK button.

Keyboard Shortcuts

The following tables list the most useful Word 97 keyboard shortcuts.

Keyboard shortcuts for editing

Shortcut	What It Does
Ctrl+X	Cuts text to the Clipboard.
Ctrl+C	Copies text to the Clipboard.
Ctrl+V	Pastes text from the Clipboard.
Ctrl+Z	Undoes the most recent command.
Ctrl+Y	Redoes an undone command.
Ctrl+Del	Deletes from the insertion point to the end of the word.
Ctrl+Backspace	Deletes from the insertion point to the start of the word.
Ctrl+F	Finds text.
Ctrl+H	Replaces occurrences of one text string with another text string.
Ctrl+A	Selects the entire document.

Keyboard shortcuts for formatting characters

Shortcut	Button	What It Does
Ctrl+B	**B**	**Bolds** text.
Ctrl+I	*I*	*Italicizes* text.
Ctrl+U	U	Underlines text (continuous).
Ctrl+Shift+W		Underlines words.
Ctrl+Shift+D		Double-underlines text.
Ctrl+Shift+A		Sets the font to ALL CAPS.
Ctrl+Shift+K		Sets the font to SMALL CAPS.
Ctrl+=		Uses subscript font.
Ctrl+Shift+=		Uses superscript font.
Ctrl+Shift+H		Makes the text hidden.
Shift+F3		Changes from uppercase to lowercase and vice versa.
Ctrl+Shift+*		Displays nonprinting characters.
Ctrl+Shift+F	A	Changes font.
Ctrl+Shift+P		Changes point size.
Ctrl+]		Increases size by one point.
Ctrl+[		Decreases size by one point.
Ctrl+Shift+>		Increases size to next available size.
Ctrl+Shift+<		Decreases size to preceding available size.
Ctrl+Shift+Q		Switches to Symbol font (Greek Tragedy).
Ctrl+Shift+Z		Removes character formatting.
Ctrl+spacebar		Removes character formatting.

Keyboard shortcuts for formatting paragraphs

Shortcut	Button	What It Does
Ctrl+L	≡	Left-aligns a paragraph.
Ctrl+R	≡	Right-aligns a paragraph.
Ctrl+J	≡	Justifies a paragraph.
Ctrl+E	≡	Centers a paragraph.

Shortcut	Button	What It Does
Ctrl+M		Increases left indent.
Ctrl+Shift+M		Reduces left indent.
Ctrl+T		Creates a hanging indent.
Ctrl+Shift+T		Reduces a hanging indent.
Ctrl+1		Single-spaces a paragraph.
Ctrl+2		Double-spaces a paragraph.
Ctrl+5		Sets line spacing to 1.5.
Ctrl+0 (zero)		Removes or sets space before a line to one line.
Ctrl+Shift+S	Normal	Applies a style.
Ctrl+K		AutoFormats.
Ctrl+Shift+N		Applies Normal style.
Ctrl+Alt+1		Applies Heading 1 style.
Ctrl+Alt+2		Applies Heading 2 style.
Ctrl+Alt+3		Applies Heading 3 style.
Ctrl+Shift+L		Applies List style.
Ctrl+Q		Removes paragraph formatting.
		Formats a numbered list.
		Formats a bullet list.

Assigning your own keyboard shortcuts

In the event that Word 97 doesn't supply enough keyboard shortcuts to fill your needs, you can easily create your own shortcuts. You can assign your own keyboard shortcuts to styles, macros, fonts, AutoText entries, commands, and symbols. Just follow these steps:

1. Choose Tools⇨Customize to open the Customize dialog box.

2. Click the Keyboard button.

The Custom Keyboard dialog box now appears as shown in the following figure:

Customize Keyboard ? ✕

Categories:

File
Edit
View
Insert
Format
Tools
Table

Commands:

FileClose
FileCloseAll
FileCloseOrCloseAll
FileConfirmConversions
FileExit
FileFind
FileNew

Close
Assign
Remove
Reset All...

Press new shortcut key:

Current keys:

Description
Closes all of the windows of the active document

Save changes in:
Normal.dot

3. Select the command, style, macro, font, or other item for which you want to create a keyboard shortcut by using the Categories and Commands lists.

4. Click the Press new shortcut key box and then type the new keyboard shortcut.

5. Click the Assign button to assign the keyboard shortcut and then click the Close button.

You can also assign keyboard shortcuts by clicking the Shortcut Key button from the dialog box that appears after you choose Insert⇨Symbol or click the Modify button in the Style dialog box, which appears after you choose Format⇨Style⇨Modify.

To reset all keyboard shortcuts to their Word 97 defaults, choose Tools⇨Customize, click the Keyboard button in the Customize dialog box to summon the Customize Keyboard dialog box, and then click the Reset All button.

Mail Merging

Mail Merge is one of the most tedious of all Word 97 tasks. Fortunately, the Mail Merge Helper stands by, ready to help you at a moment's notice. Mail Merge is a three-step process: First, you create the form letter (in Word 97 Speak, the *main document*); then you create a mailing list of names and addresses (*the data source*); and finally, you merge the form letter and the mailing list to create a letter for each person on your mailing list. The following sections spell out the procedures for each step in detail.

Creating the main document

Here's the procedure for creating a main document to use in a mail merge:

1. Choose Tools⇨Mail Merge.

The Mail Merge Helper dialog box appears.

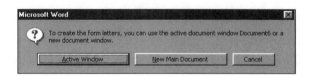

2. Click the Create button and then choose Form Letters from the drop-down list that appears.

The following dialog box appears.

3. Click the New Main Document button to open the Mail Merge Helper dialog box.

4. Click the Edit button to reveal a menu of documents you can edit.

The menu should have only one entry, Form Letter: Document #.

5. Click this selection to create the letter.

6. Type the letter any way you want, but leave blanks where you want Word 97 to insert personalized data later, such as in the inside address or the salutation (**Dear ,**).

When you edit a mail merge main document, a special Mail Merge toolbar appears above the Standard toolbar. Some of the buttons on this toolbar you use in later steps.

7. Choose File⇨Save to save the file after you're done.

Your letter should look something like the one shown here:

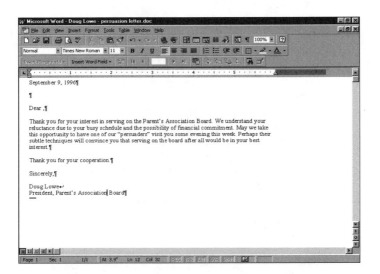

Creating the data source

The next big step in Mail Merge is creating the data source, which may be the hardest part of the procedure, because creating a data source requires you to type in all the names and addresses of those to whom you want the form letter sent. This bothersome procedure is as described in the following steps:

1. Choose Tools⇨Mail Merge.

The Mail Merge Helper dialog box returns to life.

2. Click the Get Data button and then choose Create Data Source from the menu that appears.

The Create Data Source dialog box appears.

3. To add a field, type a name in the Field name text box and then click the Add Field Name button.

4. To remove a field, click the field in the Field names in header row list to select the field and then click the Remove Field Name button.

5. To change the order in which the fields appear, select the field you want to move in the Field names in header row list and then click the up-arrow or down-arrow Move button to move the field.

6. Click the OK button after you're satisfied with the fields listed for inclusion in the data source.

The Save As dialog box appears.

7. Type an appropriate name for your mailing list document in the File name text box and then click the Save button.

A dialog box appears to inform you that the data source is empty.

8. Click the Edit Data Source button in the dialog box that appeared in Step 7 to begin adding names and addresses to the data source.

A Data Form dialog box appears, similar to the one shown in the following figure:

9. Type the information for one person you want to add to the data source.

Use the Tab key to move from field to field or to skip over those fields in which you don't want to enter any data. (You don't need to enter a value for every field.)

10. After you type all the data for the person, click the Add New button to add that person's data to the table in the data source.

11. Repeat Steps 9 and 10 for each person that you want to add to the data source.

12. After you add all the names that you want to add, click the OK button.

Notice that you can use the arrow buttons at the bottom of the Data Form dialog box to move forward or backward through the data source records. Thus you can recall a previously entered record to correct a mistake if necessary.

To delete a record, use the arrow buttons at the bottom of the Data Form dialog box to move to the record you want to delete and then click the Delete button.

Inserting field names in the main document

After you finish adding names and addresses to the data source, return to the main document. (Because the main document is still open, you can select it from the Window menu.) Now you need to add field names to the main document so that Word 97 knows where to insert data from the data source into the form letter. Here's the procedure:

1. Position the insertion point where you want to insert a field from the data source.

2. Click the Insert Merge Field button on the Mail Merge toolbar.

A menu of field names from the data source appears.

Insert Merge Field ▼
Title
FirstName
LastName
JobTitle
Company
Address1
Address2
City
State
PostalCode
Country
HomePhone
WorkPhone

3. Click the name of the field that you want to insert into the document.

4. Repeat Steps 1 through 3 for each field that you want to insert.

The following figure shows what a document looks like with all the fields inserted:

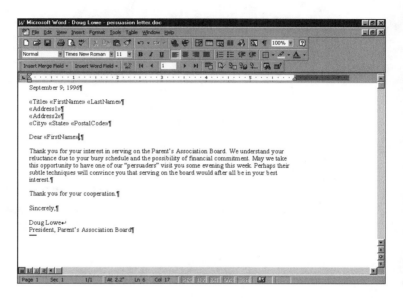

5. After you finish inserting fields, choose File⇨Save to save the file.

Merging the documents

After you set up the main document and the data source, you're ready for the show. Follow these simple steps to merge the main document with the data source to produce form letters:

1. Choose Tools⇨Mail Merge to open the Mail Merge Helper dialog box.

2. Click the Merge button.

The Merge dialog box appears.

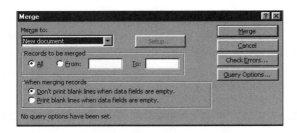

3. Click the Merge button.

Word 97 creates a new document that contains one complete copy of the main document for each record in the data source, with data from the data source substituted for each merge field. The merged copies are separated from one another by section breaks.

4. Scroll through the merged document to make sure that the merge worked the way you expected.

5. To save the merged document, choose File➪Save.

Saving the file is a good idea, but be warned that the file may be quite large, depending on how many records you merged from the data source.

6. To print the merged document, choose File➪Print.

Moving and Copying Text

The following sections describe how to move and copy text in Word 97. For more information about selecting text to be rearranged, see the section "Selecting Text," later in this part.

Dragging and dropping text

You can move text from one location to another by using the drag-and-drop technique, as follows:

1. Select the text that you want to move.

2. Place the mouse pointer anywhere over the selected text and then press and hold the left mouse button.

3. Drag the text to the location where you want to move the text.

4. Release the mouse button.

To copy rather than move text, press and hold the Ctrl key while dragging the text.

Copying text via the Clipboard

To make a duplicate copy of text, follow these steps:

1. Select the text you want to copy.

 2. Choose Edit⇨Copy, press Ctrl+C, or click the Copy button on the Standard toolbar.

3. Move the insertion point to the location where you want to insert the text.

4. Choose Edit⇨Paste, press Ctrl+V, or click the Paste button on the Standard toolbar.

Moving text via the Clipboard

To move text from one location to another, follow these steps:

1. Select the text you want to move.

2. Choose Edit⇨Cut, press Ctrl+X, or click the Cut button on the Standard toolbar.

3. Move the insertion point to the location where you want the text to appear.

4. Choose Edit⇨Paste, press Ctrl+V, or click the Paste button on the Standard toolbar.

Numbered Lists

To create a numbered list, follow this procedure:

1. Type one or more paragraphs that you want to number.

2. Select all the paragraphs that you want to number.

3. Click the Numbering button on the Formatting toolbar.

If you add or delete a paragraph in the middle of the numbered list, Word 97 renumbers the paragraphs to preserve the order. If you add a paragraph to the end of the list, Word 97 assigns the next number in sequence to the new paragraph.

The Numbering button works like a toggle: Click the button once to add numbers to paragraphs; click the button again to remove them. To remove numbering from a numbered paragraph, place the insertion point anywhere in the paragraph and click the Numbering button. To remove numbering from an entire list, select all the paragraphs in the list and click the Numbering button.

If you insert a nonnumbered paragraph in the middle of a numbered list, Word 97 breaks the list in two and begins numbering from one again for the second list. If you simply turn off numbering for one of the paragraphs in a list, however, Word 97 suspends the numbering for that paragraph and picks up where the sequence left off for the next numbered paragraph.

For more advanced numbering options, choose Format⇨Bullets and Numbering and then choose the Numbered or Outline Numbered tabs.

Replacing Text

You can choose Edit⇨Replace to replace all occurrences of one bit of text with other text. Here's the procedure:

1. Press Ctrl+Home to get to the top of the document.

If you skip this step, the search-and-replace operation starts at the position of the insertion point.

2. Choose Edit⇨Replace or press Ctrl+H to open the Find and Replace dialog box with the Replace tab active.

3. Type the text you want to find in the Find what box and then type the text you want to substitute for the Find what text in the Replace with box.

4. Click the Find Next button.

After Word 97 finds the text, the program highlights the text on-screen.

5. Click the Replace button to replace the text.

6. Repeat Steps 4 and 5 until you finish searching the document. Word 97 displays a message to tell you that it is finished.

As for the Find command, you can click the <u>M</u>ore button to display additional options such as Mat<u>c</u>h Case, Find Whole Words Onl<u>y</u>, Use Wildcards, Sounds Li<u>k</u>e, and Find All Word For<u>m</u>s options. See the section "Finding Text," earlier in this part, for details.

If you're absolutely positive that you want to replace all occurrences of your Fi<u>n</u>d what/Replace w<u>i</u>th text, click the Replace <u>A</u>ll button. This feature automatically replaces all occurrences of the text. The only problem is that you're bound to encounter at least one spot where you don't want the replacement to occur. Replacing the word *mit* with *glove*, for example, changes *Smith* to *Sgloveh.* (And no, Sgloveh is *not* the Czechoslovakian form of the name Smith.)

If you do click the Replace <u>A</u>ll button, Word 97 displays an informative message at the end of the replacement procedure, indicating how many replacements were made. If this number seems unreasonable to you (for example, you thought the document contained only three occurrences of the Fi<u>n</u>d what text, but Word 97 says that it made 257 changes), choose <u>E</u>dit➪<u>U</u>ndo to undo all the replacements in one fell swoop.

Selecting Text

You can select text in a document in many ways by using the mouse or the keyboard.

Selecting text by using the mouse

Here are the common mouse actions for selecting text:

✦ Drag the mouse over the text you want to select.

✦ Click the mouse at the start of a block of text, press and hold the Shift key, and then click again at the end of the block. This procedure selects everything in between the clicks.

✦ Double-click to select a single word.

✦ Triple-click to select an entire paragraph.

✦ Press and hold the Ctrl key and then click to select an entire sentence.

✦ Press and hold the Alt key and then drag the mouse to select any rectangular area of text.

✦ Click the selection bar (the invisible vertical area to the left of the text) to select a line.

✦ Double-click the selection bar to select an entire paragraph.

Selecting text by using the keyboard

You can use the following keyboard techniques to select text:

+ Place the cursor at the beginning of the text you want to select, press and hold the Shift key, and then move the cursor to the end of the text you want to select by using the cursor-control arrow keys. Release the Shift key after you select the text you're interested in.

+ Press Ctrl+A to select the entire document.

+ Press F8 and then press any key to extend the selection to the next occurrence of that key's character. For example, to select text from the current location to the end of a sentence, press F8 and then press the period key.

   You can keep extending the selection by pressing other keys. For example, if you press the period key again, the selection is extended to the next period. To stop extending the selection, press the Escape key.

Spell Checking

Word 97 can check your spelling in two ways. First, it can check your spelling as you type, highlighting misspelled words so that you can immediately correct them. Second, Word 97 can check your spelling after you have typed your document, enabling you to forget about spelling as you write, with the knowledge that you can correct any mistakes later on.

Spell checking as you type

Unless you disabled the Word 97 as-you-type spell checker, Word 97 spell checks your words as you type. The program underlines any misspelled words with a wavy red line.

To correct a misspelled word, click the word with the right mouse button. Then pick the correct spelling from the pop-up menu that appears.

If you don't like this automatic spell checking, you can disable the feature by following these steps:

1. Choose Tools⇨Options to open the Options dialog box.

2. Click the Spelling and Grammar tab.

3. Click the Check spelling as you type check box to deselect this option.

4. Click the OK button.

If you want to turn the automatic spell checker back on, just repeat the procedure, clicking the Check spelling as you type option to select it.

Spell checking after you type

If you disable the on-the-fly spell checking, you can always spell-check your work after the fact. Here's how:

1. Choose Tools⇨Spelling and Grammar, press F7, or click the Spelling button in the Standard toolbar.

Whichever method you choose, Word 97 begins checking your spelling from the current cursor position.

If Word 97 finds a misspelled word, the Spelling dialog box appears.

Spelling and Grammar: English (United States)	? ✕
Not in Dictionary:	
Potatoe	Ignore
	Ignore All
	Add
Suggestions:	
Potato	Change
Pottage	Change All
Potatoes	AutoCorrect
☐ Check grammar Options... Undo	Cancel

2. Depending on whether the word is misspelled, take one of the following actions:

If the word really is misspelled, select the correct spelling from the list of suggested spellings that appears in the dialog box and click the Change button. If the correct spelling doesn't appear among the suggestions, type the correct spelling in the Not in Dictionary box and click the Change button. If the word is correctly spelled, click the Ignore button. Or click the Ignore All button to ignore any subsequent occurrences of the word.

3. Repeat Step 2 until Word 97 gives up.

After Word 97 finishes with your spelling, a message appears to that effect.

Styles

Styles are one of the best ways to improve your word processing efficiency. A style is a collection of paragraph and character formats that you can apply to text in one fell swoop. The most common examples of styles are for headings. By using a style to format your headings, you can make sure that all headings are formatted in the same way. And you can quickly change the appearance of all headings by simply changing the style.

Applying a style

To apply a style to a paragraph, follow these steps:

1. Put the cursor in the paragraph you want to format.

Normal ▾

2. Select the style you want from the style box on the Formatting toolbar. (The style box is the first drop-down list box control on the Formatting toolbar.)

To apply a style to two or more adjacent paragraphs, just select a range of text that includes all the paragraphs you want to format. Then select the style.

If the style you want doesn't appear in the style list, press and hold the Shift key and then click the down arrow next to the style box. Word 97 lists only the most commonly used styles if you don't hold down the Shift key.

For more information on styles, see Chapter 14 of *Word 97 For Windows For Dummies*.

Creating a style

To create a new style, follow these steps:

1. Tweak a paragraph until the text is formatted just the way you want.

Set the font and size, line spacing, before and after spacing, and indentation. Also set tabs and any other formatting you want, such as bullets or numbers. You can set these formatting options by using either the controls on the Formatting toolbar or the commands on the Format menu.

Normal ▾

2. Click anywhere in the paragraph on which you want to base the style and then press Ctrl+Shift+S or click the style box on the Formatting toolbar.

3. Type a descriptive name for the style.

4. Press Enter to add the style to the list of styles for the document.

 Alternatively, you can choose Format⇨Style to summon the Style dialog box and then click the New button. A New Style dialog box appears that enables you to set all the formatting options for a new style.

For more information, see Chapter 14 of *Word 97 For Windows For Dummies.*

Tables of Contents

To create a table of contents, make sure that you format your document's headings by using the Word 97 heading styles (Heading 1, Heading 2, and Heading 3). If you use the heading styles, creating a table of contents is easy. Here's the procedure:

1. Move the insertion point to the place in your document where you want the table of contents to appear.

2. Choose Insert⇨Index and Tables.

The Index and Tables dialog box appears.

3. Click the Table of Contents tab.

4. Pick the Table of Contents style you want from the Formats list.

5. Play with the other controls to fine-tune the table of contents.

The following table describes the other controls of this dialog box.

Option	What It Does
Show page numbers	Deselect this check box if you want the TOC to show the document's outline but not page numbers.
Right align page numbers	Deselect this check box if you want the page numbers to be placed right next to the corresponding text rather than at the right margin.
Show levels	Use this control to set the amount of detail included in the table.
Tab leader	Select the tab leader style you want to use.

6. Click the OK button.

Word 97 inserts the TOC into your document at the insertion point.

If the table of contents looks like {TOC \o "1-3" \p " "}, choose Tools⇨Options to open the Options dialog box, click the View tab, and click the Field codes check box to remove the check mark. Click the OK button, and the table appears as it should.

If you edit a document after creating a table of contents, you can update the table of contents to make sure that its page numbers are still correct. Select the table by clicking it anywhere with the mouse and then press F9.

Tables

Tables are a nifty feature of Word 97 that enable you to organize information into a grid similar to that of a spreadsheet. Two ways are available to create tables in Word 97: the old fashioned way, by using the Table⇨Insert Table command, or the new way, which uses a fancy command called Draw Table.

Tables a la the Insert Table command

Word 97 includes a friendly Insert Table command that enables you to create tables by using any of several predefined formats. Here is the procedure:

1. Position the insertion point where you want to insert the table into your document.

2. Choose Table⇨Insert Table.

   An Insert Table dialog box appears.

3. Select the size of the table by setting the Number of columns and Number of rows text boxes.

4. Click the AutoFormat button to open the Table AutoFormat dialog box.

5. Choose the format you want to use for the table from the list of Formats.

6. Specify any other options you want to apply to the table, such as which formats to apply or whether to use special formatting for the first row or column.

7. Click the OK button to close the Table AutoFormat dialog box and then click the OK button to create the table.

After you create a table, you can type data into its cells by clicking the cell where you want to enter data and typing the data. You can use the arrow keys to move from cell to cell in any direction you want, or you can press the Tab key to move to the next cell in the table.

Alas, Microsoft dropped from Word 97 the Table Wizard, which was a part of Word for Windows 95. Apparently Microsoft decided, in its infinite wisdom, that wizardry is not required for creating tables.

Tables via the Draw Table command

New for Word 97 is a feature that enables you to draw complicated tables on-screen by using a simple set of drawing tools. The Draw Table command is ideal for creating tables that aren't merely a simple grid of rows and columns but rather boast a complex conglomeration of cells, in which some cells span more than one row and others span more than one column. These types of tables were difficult to create in Word 95, but Word 97 enables you to create such tables with just a few mouse clicks. Here's the procedure:

1. Choose Table➪Draw Table or click the Tables and Borders button on the Standard toolbar.

Word 97 switches into Page Layout View (if you aren't already there) and opens the Tables and Borders toolbar.

2. Draw the overall shape of the table by dragging the mouse to create a rectangular boundary for the table. Point the mouse where you want one of the corners of the table to be and then press and hold the mouse button while dragging the rectangle to the opposite corner.

After you release the mouse button, a table with a single cell appears, as shown in the following figure:

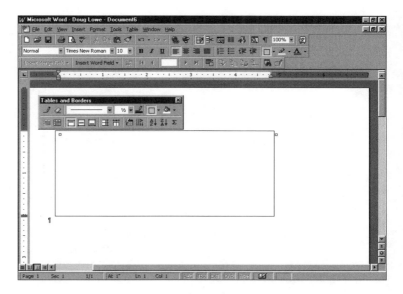

3. Carve the table up into smaller cells.

To split the table into two rows, for example, point the mouse somewhere along the left edge of the table, press and hold the mouse button, and then drag a line across the table to the right edge. After you release the mouse, the table splits into two rows, as shown in the following figure:

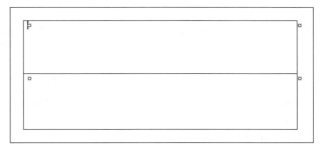

You can continue to carve up the table into smaller and smaller cells. For each slice, point the mouse at one edge of where you want the new cell to begin and drag the mouse to the other edge. If you want to change the line size or style drawn for a particular segment, you can use the line style and size drop-down controls in the Tables and Borders toolbar. You can change the style of a line you've already drawn by tracing over the line with a new style. The following figure shows some of the possibilities available in creating your table:

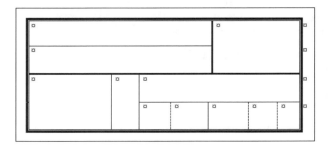

4. After you finish creating your table, click the Tables and Borders button again to close the Tables and Borders toolbar.

You can then type data into any of the table's cells by clicking the cell to select it and typing the data.

Tabs

The following sections list the most common procedures for working with tabs.

Setting tabs

Here's the procedure for setting tabs by using the ruler, which sits atop the document window. (If the ruler isn't visible, use the View⇨Ruler command to reveal it.) Follow these steps:

1. Type some text that you want to line up with tab stops.

2. Select the paragraph or paragraphs for which you want to set tabs.

3. Click the ruler at each spot where you want a new tab stop.

4. Adjust the settings until you like the way the text looks.

To adjust a tab setting, just use the mouse to grab the tab marker in the ruler and slide the tab to the new location. (If you can't find the ruler, choose View⇨Ruler.) After you release the mouse button, text in the currently selected paragraphs adjusts to the new tab position.

Default tab stops lie every .5 inch in the ruler. Each time you create a new tab stop, however, Word 97 deletes all default tab stops to the left of the new tab stop. In other words, default tab stops continue to exist only to the right of new tab stops you create.

Word 97 enables you to create four types of tab alignments: *left*, *center*, *right*, and *decimal*. To change the type of tab that you created as you click the ruler, click the Tab Alignment button at the far-left edge of the ruler. Each time you click this button, the picture on the button changes to indicate the alignment type, as follows:

✦ **Left tab:** Text left-aligns at the tab stop.

✦ **Center tab:** Text centers over the tab stop.

✦ **Right tab:** Text right-aligns at the tab stop.

✦ **Decimal tab:** Numbers align at the decimal point over the tab stop.

To remove a tab stop from the ruler, click the tab stop you want to remove and drag the tab off the ruler. After you release the mouse button, the tab stop disappears.

To quickly remove all tab stops, choose Format➪Tabs and then click the Clear All button in the Tabs dialog box.

For more information, see Chapter 10 of *Word 97 For Windows For Dummies*.

Creating leader tabs

Leader tabs have rows of dots instead of spaces between tab stops. (Leader tabs are common in tables of contents and indexes.) Here's the procedure for creating leader tabs:

1. Set a tab stop by using the procedure described in the section "Setting Tab Stops."

2. Choose Format➪Tabs.

The Tabs dialog box appears.

3. Choose the leader style by selecting option <u>2</u>, <u>3</u>, or <u>4</u> in the Leader area.

4. Click the OK button.

Now, after you press the Tab key, a row of dots or a solid line appears.

For more information, see Chapter 10 of *Word 97 For Windows For Dummies.*

Templates

Suppose that you toiled for hours on a document, and now you want to make its styles, macros, and other goodies available to other documents you may someday create. You can do that by creating a *template*. Then, if you create a new document based on your template, that document inherits the styles, AutoText entries (portions of prerecorded text that you can call up with just a few mouse clicks), macros, and text from the template. Here's how to create a template:

1. Open the document that has all the styles, AutoText, macros, and other goodies you want to save in a template.

2. Choose <u>F</u>ile⇨Save <u>A</u>s to open the Save As dialog box.

3. In the Save as <u>t</u>ype list box (way down at the bottom of the Save As dialog box), select Document Template as the file type.

4. In the File <u>n</u>ame text box, type a filename for the template.

(Don't type the extension; Word 97 takes care of that element.)

5. Click the <u>S</u>ave button to save the document as a template file.

6. Delete any unnecessary text from the file.

(Any text that you do not delete automatically appears in any new documents you create based on the template.)

7. Save the file again.

You can also create a template by choosing <u>F</u>ile⇨<u>N</u>ew and then clicking the <u>T</u>emplate radio button in the New dialog box. Doing so creates an empty template based on the template you select in the dialog box. You can then modify the template as you see fit and save that template under a new name.

For more information, see Chapter 15 of *Word 97 For Windows For Dummies.*

Web Page Wizard

Word 97 comes with a slick Web Page Wizard that can automatically create several different types of Web documents based on options you select. To use the Wizard, follow these steps:

1. Choose File⇔New.

2. After the New dialog box appears, click the Web Pages tab, click Web Page Wizard, and then click the OK button.

The Web Page Wizard dialog box appears.

3. Choose from the list the type of Web page you want to create.

The Web Wizard offers about a dozen different types of pages.

4. Click the Next button.

The Wizard asks which of several visual styles you want to use for your page. Each style uses a different background, text formats and colors, and line and bullet styles. The example in the following figure shows how a page looks using the Community style:

5. Click the Finish button to create the page.

6. Make any modifications you want.

You need to make plenty of changes, because the page initially consists of little more than placeholders such as Insert Heading Here and Click here to add text.

7. Choose File⇨Save As to save the file using whatever name you want.

Web Toolbar

One of the coolest new features of Word 97 is the Web toolbar. This toolbar enables you to more easily browse Office 97 documents that are linked together with hyperlinks and to browse the Internet's World Wide Web. The Web toolbar is shown in the following figure:

To access the Web toolbar, choose View⇨Toolbars to open the Toolbars dialog box. Click Web to select the Web toolbar and then click the OK button.

At the far right of the Web toolbar is a list box in which you can type the filename of a file you want to open or the URL of an Internet address you would like to visit. The following table describes the other buttons in the Web toolbar:

Button	What It Does
⇦	Displays the previous page.
⇨	Displays the next page in sequence.
⊗	Cancels a download in process.
🗐	Obtains a new copy of the document or HTML page.
🏠	Takes you to your start page, which you designated in Internet Explorer 3.0 as the first page to display after you enter the Internet.
🔍	Calls up a search page that enables you to search the Internet for specific information.
Favorites ▾	Displays a list of your favorite documents so that you can quickly access them. Also includes an Add to Favorites command so that you can add items to your Favorites menu.
Go ▾	Displays a menu that lists the same commands previously described for the Web toolbar.
🔼	Shows only the Web toolbar so that more space is available to display the document.

Part IV

Excel 97

Excel 97 is the bean-counter of Microsoft Office 97. It enables you to create spreadsheets that can perform meticulous calculations with uncanny accuracy. This part covers the basics of using Excel 97. If you're interested in going beyond the basics, you can find more information in *Excel 97 For Windows For Dummies,* by Greg Harvey, published by IDG Books Worldwide, Inc.

In this part . . .

✔ **The most useful Excel 97 functions**

✔ **Formatting cells**

✔ **Working with Pivot Tables**

✔ **Creating great-looking charts**

✔ **Keyboard shortcuts for common Excel 97 tasks**

✔ **Saving your worksheet as HTML code**

AutoFormatting

You can efficiently create an attractively formatted worksheet by using the AutoFormat feature to apply predefined formatting to your worksheet. Here's how:

1. Create your worksheet as you normally would.

The AutoFormat feature works best when the first row and the first column of the worksheet contain headings and the last row contains totals, as many of the AutoFormats apply special formatting to the first row and column. The last column of the worksheet may also contain totals, but it doesn't have to. The AutoFormats work whether or not the last column contains totals. They also work if the first row and column do not contain headings, but you may have to remove the special formatting for the first row and column.

2. Highlight the entire range of worksheet cells that contains data you want to format, as shown in the following figure:

3. Choose Format⇨AutoFormat.

The AutoFormat dialog box appears, as shown in the following figure:

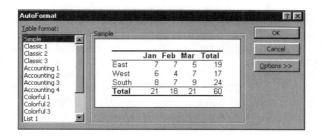

4. Select the <u>T</u>able format you want to use from the list in the dialog box.

A preview of each AutoFormat you select appears in the Sample portion of the AutoFormat dialog box.

5. Click the OK button.

Excel 97 applies the selected AutoFormat to your worksheet, as shown in the following figure:

If you don't like the formatting applied by the AutoFormat, press Ctrl+Z or choose <u>E</u>dit➪<u>U</u>ndo to undo the AutoFormat operation.

Centering Text over Several Columns

You may frequently want to center text over several columns. Suppose, for example, that you put projected net sales for 1994, 1995, and 1996 in columns B, C, and D, respectively, and actual net sales for 1994, 1995, and 1996 in columns E, F, and G. Wouldn't having a Projected Net Sales heading centered over the projected net sales columns and an Actual Net Sales heading centered over the actual net sales columns be a really nice touch?

You can accomplish this effect by merging cells from the three columns to create a single cell that spans several columns. Here is the procedure:

1. Move the cell pointer to the leftmost cell in the range of columns over which you want to center the text.

For example, if you want text centered over the range B3:D3, move the cell pointer to cell B3. (See the section "Referencing Spreadsheet Cells," later in this part, if the notation B3:D3 confuses you.)

2. Enter the text that you want to center into the cell you have selected.

3. Highlight the range of cells across which you want the text centered.

The worksheet should look something like the one shown in the following figure:

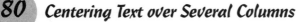

	A	B	C	D	E	F	G	H	I	J
1				Sales Budget Comparison 1994-1996						
2		Projected Net Sales			Actual Net Sales					
3		1994	1995	1996	1994	1995	1996			
4	Northwest	3,500.00	3,750.00	4,000.00	2,874.00	3,726.00	3,788.00			
5	Southwest	5,000.00	5,500.00	6,000.00	4,873.00	5,878.00	6,499.00			
6	Northeast	4,000.00	4,250.00	4,500.00	3,888.00	5,390.00	4,104.00			
7	Southeast	4,500.00	4,500.00	4,500.00	4,513.00	4,578.00	4,602.00			
8										
9	Total	$17,000.00	$18,000.00	$19,000.00	$16,148.00	$19,572.00	$18,993.00			

4. Click the Merge and Center button.

The result should look like the example shown in the following figure. (In this example, both the Projected Net Sales and the Actual Net Sales headings are centered.)

	A	B	C	D	E	F	G	H
1			Sales Budget Comparison 1994-1996					
2			Projected Net Sales		Actual Net Sales			
3		1994	1995	1996	1994	1995	1996	
4	Northwest	3,500.00	3,750.00	4,000.00	2,874.00	3,726.00	3,788.00	
5	Southwest	5,000.00	5,500.00	6,000.00	4,873.00	5,878.00	6,499.00	
6	Northeast	4,000.00	4,250.00	4,500.00	3,888.00	5,390.00	4,104.00	
7	Southeast	4,500.00	4,500.00	4,500.00	4,513.00	4,578.00	4,602.00	
8								
9	Total	$17,000.00	$18,000.00	$19,000.00	$16,148.00	$19,572.00	$18,993.00	

If you change your mind and don't want to center the text across columns, highlight the merged cell, choose Format⇨Cells to bring up the Format Cells dialog box, and deselect the Merge Cells check box on the Alignment tab.

Charting

Excel 97 offers so many charting capabilities that I could write an entire Quick Reference just on charting. Here's the short procedure for quickly creating a simple chart:

1. Select the cells that contain the data on which you want to base a chart.

 2. Click the ChartWizard button on the Standard toolbar.

The Chart Wizard comes to life, as shown in the following figure:

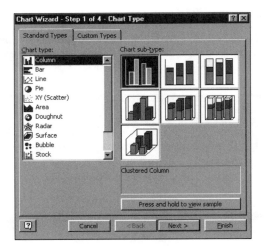

3. Select from the Chart type list the type of chart you want to create.

For each chart type, you can choose from several subtypes. To see a preview of how the selected data appears charted with a particular chart type, select that chart type from the list and click and hold the mouse button on the Press and hold to view sample button.

4. Click the Next button.

The following version of this dialog box appears:

5. Check the range shown in the Data range box to verify that the range listed is the range you want to chart.

The Chart Wizard initially assumes that the data you are trying to chart is grouped by row. In other words, the first row of the range contains the first series of values, the second row contains the second series, and so on. If this isn't the case, you can click the Columns radio button so that the data is grouped by column, with the first data series in the first column of the range, the second series in the second column, and so on.

6. Click the Next button.

The following version of this dialog box appears:

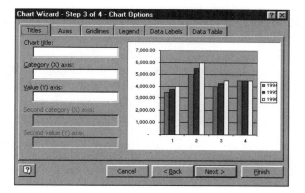

7. Add any optional features to your chart by filling in the text boxes and setting various option buttons that appear on the Chart Options version of the Chart Wizard dialog box. Notice that the Chart Options dialog box has six tabs that display various charting options. Be sure to check the settings on all six tabs before proceeding.

For example, you can include a title for the chart by typing a title into the Chart title text box.

The changes you make to the settings on the Chart Options dialog box appear in the preview area, which takes up the entire right side of the dialog box. This preview gives you an idea of how each setting affects the chart's appearance.

8. Click the Next button.

The Chart Wizard displays its final dialog box.

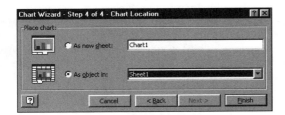

9. Choose where you want Excel 97 to place your chart — as a new sheet or as an object in any sheet in the current workbook — and then click the Finish button to create the chart.

If you added the chart to an existing sheet, you may need to drag and possibly resize the chart to its correct location and size.

Comments

Excel 97 enables you to add an electronic version of those yellow sticky notes to your worksheets. You can use this feature as a reminder to yourself and others who may use the worksheet, such as why you created a formula the way you did or where you got a particular number you entered into the worksheet. Just follow these steps:

1. Click the cell to which you want to add the note.

2. Choose Insert⇨Comment or press Shift+F2.

A yellow, balloon-style box appears.

3. Type anything you want in the box.

You can, for example, question the value listed in the cell, as shown in the following figure:

4. Click anywhere outside the yellow comment balloon.

The comment balloon disappears, and Excel 97 adds a colored marker to the cell to indicate that a comment is attached to that cell. To access the comment later, simply point to the cell; the comment balloon appears. The balloon disappears after you move the mouse away from the cell.

To delete a comment, right-click the cell and choose Delete Comment from the pop-up menu that appears.

Finding Lost Data

You can choose Edit⇨Find to find text anywhere in a worksheet. Just follow these steps:

1. Press Ctrl+Home to move to the top of the worksheet.

This step is optional; if you omit it, the search starts at the current cell.

2. Use the Edit⇨Find command or press Ctrl+F to summon the Find dialog box.

3. Type the text you want to find in the Find what text box.

4. Click the Find Next button.

When Excel 97 finds the cell that contains the text you're looking for, it highlights the cell. The Find dialog box remains on-screen so that you can click Find Next to find yet another occurrence of the text.

After Excel 97 finds the last occurrence of the text, it resumes its search again from the top. This process goes on forever, until you bail out by clicking Cancel or pressing Esc.

The Find dialog box offers several options for controlling the search, as described in the following table.

Option	What It Does
Search	Indicates whether you want to search by rows or columns.
Look in	Indicates whether you want to search cell values, formulas, or notes attached to cells.
Match case	Finds only text with the case (uppercase and lowercase letters) that matches the search text you type.
Find entire cells only	Finds text only if the entire cell entry matches the Find what text.

You can use the following wildcard characters in the Find what text box:

✦ ? finds a single occurrence of any character. For example, **f?t** finds *fat* and *fit*.

✦ * finds any combination of characters. For example, **b*t** finds any combination of characters that begins with *b* and ends with *t*, such as *bat, bait, ballast,* and *bacteriologist.*

If you find the text you're looking for and decide that you want to replace it with something else, click Replace. This action opens the Replace dialog box.

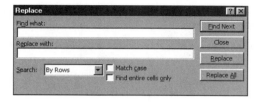

You can then type replacement text in the Replace with text box, and then click Replace to replace a single occurrence of the Find text or Replace All to replace the Find text wherever it appears in the document.

Formatting a Cell or Range of Cells

You can set formats for a cell or range of cells by using the formatting keyboard shortcuts listed in the section "Keyboard Shortcuts for Formatting Cells," later in this part, or by using the formatting controls on the Formatting toolbar. Or you can use the following procedure to apply character formats by using the Format⇨Cells command:

1. Highlight the cell or cells to which you want to apply the formatting.

2. Choose Format⇨Cells or use the handy keyboard shortcut, Ctrl+1.

Either way, the Format Cells dialog box appears, as shown in the following figure:

3. Play with the controls under the six tabs to set the formatting options that you want.

4. Click the OK button after you format the cells the way you want.

Formula AutoCorrect Functions

The following list details some common Excel 97 functions. The program has hundreds of other functions that you can use, but these are the most common. For information on how to insert a function, see the section "The Function Wizard," later in this part.

ABS

ABS(*number*)

Returns the absolute value of *number*. *Number* is usually a cell reference, as in ABS(B3), or the result of a calculation, such as ABS(D19-D17).

AVERAGE

AVERAGE(*range*)

Calculates the average value of the cells in *range* by determining the sum of all the cells and then dividing the result by the number of cells in the range. Excel 97 doesn't count blank cells, but the program does count cells that contain the value zero.

COUNT

COUNT(*range*)

Returns the number of cells in *range*. Excel 97 doesn't count blank cells, but the program does count cells that contain the value zero.

HLOOKUP

HLOOKUP(*lookup_value, table_array, row_index_num*)

Searches for the cell in *table_array* that contains the value specified by *lookup_value*. HLOOKUP searches all the cells in the first row of the range specified for *table_array*. If the function finds *lookup_value,* HLOOKUP returns the value of the corresponding cell in the row indicated by *row_index_num*. To return the value in the corresponding cell in the second row of the table, for example, specify **2** for *row_index_num*.

IF

IF(*logical_test, value_if_true, value_if_false*)

Tests the condition specified in the logical test. If the condition is true, Excel 97 returns *value_if_true*. Otherwise, the program returns *value_if_false*.

LOWER

LOWER(*text*)

Converts the *text* to lowercase.

MAXIMUM

MAXIMUM(*range*)

Returns the largest value in *range*.

MEDIAN

MEDIAN(*range*)

Returns the median value of the cells in *range*. If you sort the cells in order, the median value is the value in the cell that falls right in the middle of the sorted list. Half the cell values are larger than the median value, and the other half are smaller.

MINIMUM

MINIMUM(*range*)

Returns the smallest value in *range*.

NOW

NOW()

Returns the current date and time. No arguments are required.

PMT

PMT(*rate, nper, pv*)

Calculates payments for a loan. *Rate* is the interest rate per period; *nper* is the number of periods; *pv* is the present value (that is, the amount of the loan). Make sure that you specify the interest rate for each period and the total number of periods. If, for example, the annual interest rate is 12 percent and you make payments monthly, the periodic interest rate is 1 percent. Likewise, if the loan is for three years and you make payments monthly, 36 periods exist.

As an example, suppose you want to know the payments for a 48-month loan of $15,000 at 7 percent. The PMT function should be PMT(7%/12,48,15000).

PRODUCT

PRODUCT(*range*)

Multiplies all the cells in the specified *range*.

PROPER

PROPER(*text*)

Converts the text to proper case, in which the program capitalizes the first letter of each word in *text*.

ROUND

ROUND(*number, decimal places*)

Rounds off the number to the specified number of decimal places. For example, ROUND(C1,2) rounds off the value in cell C1 to two decimal places.

SUM

SUM(*range*)

Adds the values of all cells in the specified range.

SUMPRODUCT

SUMPRODUCT(*range1, range2*)

Multiplies each cell in *range1* by its corresponding cell in *range2* and then adds the resulting products together.

TODAY

TODAY()

Returns the current date. No arguments are required.

UPPER

UPPER(*text*)

Converts the *text* to uppercase.

VLOOKUP

VLOOKUP(*lookup_value*, *table_array*, *col_index_num*)

Searches for the cell in *table_array* that contains the value specified by *lookup_value*. VLOOKUP searches all the cells in the first column of the range specified for *table_array*. If the function finds *lookup_value*, VLOOKUP returns the value of the corresponding cell in the column indicated by *col_index_num*. To return the value in the corresponding cell in the second column of the table, for example, specify **2** for *col_index_num*.

The Function Wizard

The easiest way to insert a function is to use the Function Wizard. The Function Wizard asks you to select a function from one of several function categories and to complete the function by providing all the information the function requires.

Here's the procedure, using a simple MAX function as an example:

1. Move the cell pointer to the cell in which you want to insert the function.

2. Choose Insert⇨Function.

The Paste Function dialog box appears. The Paste Function dialog box initially lists the functions you used most recently.

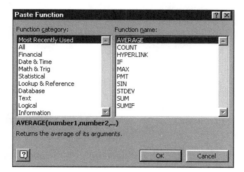

3. If the function that you want to insert in the cell appears in the Function name list, click to select the name of the function; otherwise, click one of the categories in the Function category list and then select the function from the Function name list.

4. Click the OK button.

A dialog box appears, similar to the one in the following figure:

5. Read the instructions for completing the function and then type whatever entries you need to complete the function.

If the function requires just a single argument, Excel 97 uses the cell or range that was selected at the time you accessed the Function Wizard. This means that you don't need to do anything in this dialog box except click the OK button.

If the function requires more than one argument, you can type a value, cell reference, or a range into the text boxes for the additional arguments. If you want, you can mark a cell or range of cells in the spreadsheet by clicking the button that appears to the right of the text box for the argument you want to enter. This action returns you to the spreadsheet, where you can mark the cell or range. Press Enter to return to the Function Wizard; the range you marked appears in the text box for the argument.

6. Click the OK button after you complete the function.

For more information about specific functions, see the section "Functions," earlier in this part.

Hyperlinks

Excel 97 enables you to designate a cell as a hyperlink that, after you click it, opens another document. A hyperlink can open another file, such as an Excel 97 spreadsheet or a Word 97 document, or the hyperlink can also open an Internet address (URL) that retrieves and displays a page on the Word Wide Web.

To create a hyperlink in an Excel 97 spreadsheet, follow these steps:

1. Select the cell that you want to turn into a hyperlink.

2. Choose Insert⇨Hyperlink.

The Insert Hyperlink dialog box appears, as shown in the following figure:

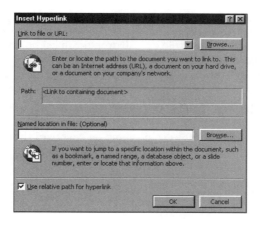

3. Type the Internet address (URL) in the Link to file or URL drop-down list box.

To link to another file that's a part of your own Web site, just type the filename (for example, **SOMEFILE.HTM**). To link to a page at another site, type the complete URL (for example, `http://www.somewhere.com/somepage.htm`).

To link to another Office 97 document rather than an Internet site, just type the name of the file.

You can also click the Browse button to search for the file on disk.

4. To link to a specific location within a file, type the name of the location in the Named location in file text box.

The following table lists how named locations apply to documents created with Microsoft Office 97 applications.

Type of Document	*How Named Locations Apply*
Word 97 document	Bookmarks (Insert⇨Bookmark)
Excel 97 worksheet	Range names (Insert⇨Name)
PowerPoint 97 presentation	Slide number (each slide in a presentation is automatically assigned a slide number)
Access 97 database	Any named database object, such as a table or query

5. Click the OK button.

TIP

You can use hyperlinks to provide a quick way to jump to a named range within the current spreadsheet. To do that, choose Insert⇨ Hyperlink, leave the Link to file or URL drop-down list box blank, and then enter the name of the range you want to link to in the Named location in file text box.

Keyboard Shortcuts for Editing

The following table describes some common keyboard shortcuts for editing data in Excel 97.

Shortcut	What It Does
Ctrl+X	Cuts text to the Clipboard.
Ctrl+C	Copies text to the Clipboard.
Ctrl+V	Pastes text from the Clipboard.
Ctrl+Z	Undoes the last action.
Ctrl+F	Opens a dialog box for finding text.
Ctrl+H	Opens a dialog box for replacing text.
Ctrl+A	Selects everything in a worksheet.
Ctrl+D	Fills the selected range of cells downward, using the values at the top of the range to determine the sequence of values to use.
Ctrl+R	Fills the selected range of cells to the right, using the values at the left of the range to determine the sequence of values to use.
Ctrl+;	Enters the current date.
Ctrl+Shift+:	Enters the current time.

Keyboard Shortcuts for Formatting Cells

The following table describes common keyboard shortcuts for formatting cell data in Excel 97.

Shortcut	What It Does
Ctrl+1	Opens the Format Cells dialog box so that you can apply cell formatting.
Ctrl+B	**Bolds** selected text.
Ctrl+I	*Italicizes* selected text.
Ctrl+U	Underlines selected text.
Ctrl+Shift+~	Applies general number style.
Ctrl+Shift+$	Applies currency number style.
Ctrl+Shift+%	Applies percent number style.

Shortcut	What It Does
Ctrl+Shift+ ^	Applies exponential number style.
Ctrl+Shift+ #	Applies date number style.
Ctrl+Shift+ @	Applies time number style.
Ctrl+Shift+ !	Applies comma number style.
Ctrl+Shift+ &	Adds an outline border.
Ctrl+Shift+ _	Removes outline borders.

Keyboard Shortcuts for Selecting Cells

The following table describes the keyboard shortcuts used for selecting cells in Excel 97.

Shortcut	What It Does
Ctrl+spacebar	Selects the entire column.
Shift+spacebar	Selects the entire row.
Ctrl+Shift+spacebar	Selects the entire worksheet.
Ctrl+A	Selects the entire worksheet.
Ctrl+Shift+*	Selects the entire block of data.
Ctrl+Shift+?	Selects all cells that have a note attached.

Moving Around

You can move around a worksheet easily enough by using the mouse; just click the cell you want to move to. See the section "Using the IntelliMouse" in Part II for more information on moving around with the mouse.

The following table summarizes the keyboard techniques you can use for moving around a worksheet.

Shortcut	What It Does
Home	Moves to the beginning of the current row.
PgUp	Scrolls the window up one screen.
PgDn	Scrolls the window down one screen.
Alt+PgDn	Scrolls the window right one screen.
Alt+PgUp	Scrolls the window left one screen.

(continued)

Shortcut	What It Does
Ctrl+End	Moves to the last cell of the worksheet that contains data.
Ctrl+Home	Moves to the beginning of the worksheet.
Ctrl+← or End, ←	Moves to the left of a data block.
Ctrl+→ or End, →	Moves to the right of a data block.
Ctrl+↑ or End, ↑	Moves to the top of a data block.
Ctrl+↓ or End, ↓	Moves to the bottom of a data block.
Ctrl+PgUp	Switches to the preceding sheet in the same workbook.
Ctrl+PgDn	Switches to the next sheet in the same workbook.
End, Home	Moves to the last cell in the worksheet that contains data.
End, Enter	Moves to the last cell in the current row that contains data.
Ctrl+G	Goes to a specific location.

Naming a Range of Cells

To make your formulas easier to understand, Excel 97 enables you to assign meaningful names to individual cells or cell ranges. Here's the procedure for assigning a name to a cell or range of cells:

1. Select the cell or range of cells to which you want to assign a name.

2. Choose Insert⇨Name⇨Define to open the Define Name dialog box, as shown in the following figure:

```
Define Name                              ? X
Names in workbook:
[                            ]          [   OK    ]
┌──────────────────────────┐▲          [  Close  ]
│                          │            [   Add   ]
│                          │            [  Delete ]
│                          │
│                          │
│                          │▼
Refers to:
[=Sheet1!$C$13:$C$14                    ]
```

3. Type a name for the cell or cell range in the Names in workbook text box.

4. Click the OK button to close the Define Name dialog box.

To use a range name in a formula, type the name anytime you would type a range. Instead of typing **=Sum(F4:F15)**, for example, you can type the formula **=Sum(SalesTotals)**.

To delete a range name, choose Insert⇨Name⇨Define to open the Define Name dialog box, select the range name that you want to delete from the list, and then click the Delete button.

You can quickly select a named range by either pressing F5 or choosing Edit⇨Go To to open the Go To dialog box and then double-clicking the range name in the list box.

Pivot Tables

A *pivot table* is a slick way of summarizing information that is stored in an Excel 97 worksheet or an Access 97 database. You can use pivot tables with worksheets in which information is stored in rows, where each column represents a field.

Suppose, for example, that you are charged with tracking fund-raising activities of a group of students. Each row in a worksheet can represent a single fund-raising activity for a particular student, with columns for the student's name, the fund-raising activity, the amount raised, and the month in which the activity occurred. Such a worksheet may look like the example in the following figure:

To create a pivot table from a worksheet such as this, follow these steps:

1. Select a cell within the worksheet's table that you want to serve as the basis for the pivot table.

   Which cell you select doesn't matter, as long as the cell is within the table on the worksheet.

2. Choose Data➪PivotTable Report to open the PivotTable Wizard, as shown in the following figure:

3. Leave the data source option set to Microsoft Excel List or Database and click the Next button to proceed.

   Step 2 of the PivotTable Wizard appears, as shown in the following figure. If you selected a cell within the table before starting the PivotTable Wizard, Excel 97 should correctly guess the range of cells on which to base the pivot table. If not, you can change it here.

4. If the correct range appears in the Range text box, click Next to move on to Step 3 of the PivotTable Wizard, as shown in the following figure:

PivotTable Wizard - Step 3 of 4

Construct your PivotTable by dragging the field buttons on the right to the diagram on the left.

PAGE   COLUMN

ROW   DATA

Student
Fund Rais
Amount
Month

Cancel   < Back   Next >   Finish

Each column in the table appears as a field button in the PivotTable Wizard.

5. Pick the field that contains the data you want to summarize and drag the button for that field into the Data area of the pivot table.

In the Fund Raising table, for example, you drag the Amount field to the Data area.

6. Drag the other fields to the Row, Column, or Page areas, depending on how you want to summarize the data. For the Fund Raising example, I dragged the Student button to the Column area, the Fund Raiser button to the Row area, and the Month button to the Page area.

After Excel 97 creates the pivot table, you can move these fields around to change how Excel 97 summarizes the data. Here's how the PivotTable Wizard may appear after the fields have been dragged into the pivot table:

PivotTable Wizard - Step 3 of 4

Construct your PivotTable by dragging the field buttons on the right to the diagram on the left.

Month
PAGE   Fund Rais

Student   COLUMN

Sum of Amount

ROW   DATA

Student
Fund Rais
Amount
Month

Cancel   < Back   Next >   Finish

7. Click the Next button to continue.

The final step of the Pivot Wizard appears, as shown in the following figure:

PivotTable Wizard - Step 4 of 4

Where do you want to put the PivotTable?

- New worksheet
- Existing worksheet

Click Finish to create your PivotTable.

Cancel   Options...   < Back   Next >   Finish

8. Leave the New worksheet radio button selected so that Excel 97 creates the pivot table in its own worksheet and then click the Finish button to create the pivot table.

Here's how the pivot table should look after Excel 97 finishes its work:

	A	B	C	D	E	F	G	H
1	Month	(All)						
2								
3	Sum of Amount	Student						
4	Fund Raiser	Bart Simpson	D.J. Tanner	Jane Banks	Jethro Bodine	Marcia Brady	Opie Taylor	Steven Q. L
5	Candy	57	89	75	89	56	86	
6	Dance	92	86	25	12	78	42	
7	Fund Run	13	46	75	90	46	34	
8	Scrip	267	49	60	101	100	177	
9	Silent Auction	57	156	60	123	35	56	
10	T-Shirts	13	46	30	67	34	90	
11	Grand Total	499	472	325	482	349	485	

You can change how Excel 97 summarizes the pivot table's information by dragging the field buttons to different locations in the table. If, for example, you'd rather see each student's fund-raising activities summarized by month, drag the fields around so that the table appears as shown in the following figure:

Printing a Worksheet

Printing in Excel 97 is pretty much the same as printing in any other Office 97 application: You can choose File⇔Print, press Ctrl+P, or click the Print button in the Standard toolbar to print the current worksheet. Excel 97, however, offers a few printing tricks that you should know about:

+ By default, Excel 97 prints the entire worksheet. However, you can set a print area to print just part of the worksheet. First, highlight the range you want to print. Then choose File⇔Print Area⇔Set Print Area.

+ To clear the print area so that the entire worksheet prints, choose File⇔Print Area⇔Clear Print Area.

+ If annoying grid lines appear on your printed output, choose File⇔Page Setup to summon the Page Setup dialog box. Click the Sheet tab and then click Gridlines to remove the check mark. Click the OK button to dismiss the Page Setup dialog box.

Referencing Spreadsheet Cells

Like other spreadsheet programs, Excel 97 uses a standard notation to refer to cells within a worksheet. Each column in a worksheet is assigned a letter — A, B, C, and so on. Columns beyond column Z use two letters, so the columns that come next after column Z are columns AA, AB, AC, and so on. Rows are numbered, starting with 1.

Each cell is given an *address* that is a combination of its column letter and row number. Thus the cell at the intersection of column E and row 5 is cell E5.

A *range* of cells is a rectangular area that is identified by two cells at opposite corners, separated by a colon. Thus the range C7:E10 is all the cells in a rectangle with its upper left corner at cell C7 and lower right corner at E10.

You sometimes see cell addresses that use dollar signs ($), such as D$9, $E7, or $H$22. The dollar sign designates the row or column portion of an address as *absolute,* meaning that Excel 97 shouldn't try to adjust the address if you move or copy a formula that includes the absolute address. For example, suppose that you type the formula =**D3+D4** into cell D5 and then copy cell D5 to cell E5; Excel 97 adjusts the formula to =E3+E4. But if you make the formula in cell D5 =**$D3+$D4**, Excel 97 does *not* adjust the formula if you copy it to another column.

One new trick for Excel 97 is that the program can use labels that appear above a column of numbers as cell addresses. For example, suppose you set up a spreadsheet as shown in the following example:

	A	B	C
1	Cost	Quantity	
2	14.95	3	
3			
4			
5			
6			
7			

To create a formula in cell C2 that multiplies cells A2 and B2, you could enter =**A2*B2**. With Excel 97, however, you can enter the formula as =**Cost*Quantity**. Excel uses the column headings in row 1 to figure out that *Cost* is cell A2 and *Quantity* is cell B2.

Saving as HTML

Excel 97 includes a new Save as HTML command that converts an Excel 97 worksheet to an HTML table that you can publish on the World Wide Web. Here's the procedure for using this command:

1. Open the worksheet you want to convert to HTML.

2. Select the portion of the worksheet you want to convert to HTML. For example, in the following figure, the range A1:D9 is selected:

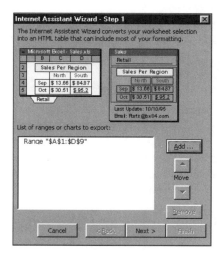

3. Choose File⇨Save as HTML to summon the Internet Assistant Wizard, as shown in the following figure:

4. Click the Next button to display Step 2 of the Internet Assistant Wizard, as shown here:

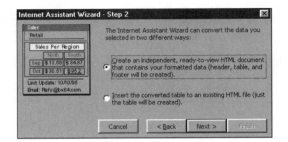

This dialog box gives you two options for converting your worksheet to HTML. The first option (and the one that is described here) creates a complete HTML document that displays your data. The second option inserts HTML codes for your worksheet into an HTML document you previously created.

5. Click the Next button to proceed to Step 3 of the Internet Assistant Wizard, as shown here:

6. Complete the formatting information requested in Step 3 of the Internet Assistant Wizard by typing a title, header, and description for your worksheet data and indicating whether you want horizontal lines inserted before or after the worksheet data.

7. Click Next to summon Step 4 of the Internet Assistant Wizard.

8. In the File Path text box, type a filename and path for the HTML document that you want to create.

9. Click the Finish button to create the HTML document.

After grinding and churning for a moment, the Internet Assistant Wizard successfully completes its work, and you have a Web page ready to be displayed on the World Wide Web.

Part V

PowerPoint 97

If you like to stand in front of a group of people with a flip chart and a pointer, either trying to get them to buy something from you or convincing them to vote for you, you'll love PowerPoint 97. PowerPoint 97 creates presentations that can be printed out on plain paper or made into transparencies or slides, or shown on-screen as an online presentation.

This part shows how to perform the most common PowerPoint 97 chores. For more complete information about using PowerPoint 97, get a copy of my book, *PowerPoint 97 For Windows For Dummies,* published by IDG Books Worldwide, Inc.

In this part . . .

✔ **Using transitions and build effects to create animated slides**

✔ **Working with color**

✔ **Using the PowerPoint 97 Viewer**

✔ **Finding lost slides**

✔ **Creating notes**

✔ **Adding clip art**

✔ **Publishing your presentation on the Web**

Animation

Animation allows you to add movement to your slides, which can help keep your audience awake. Every object on a slide can have its own animation effect. You can control the order in which objects are animated and whether animations are manually controlled or happen automatically after a certain time has passed. To add animation to your presentation, follow these steps:

1. Switch to Slide View and scroll to the slide you want to animate.

2. Choose Slide Show➪Custom Animation. The Custom Animation dialog box appears.

3. Set your options on the Timing tab. Click the slide element you want to animate (such as Title or Text) and then click the Animate radio button.

If you want the animation to occur automatically, click Automatically and then set the number of seconds you want to pass before the animation starts. If you want the animation to occur when the user clicks the mouse, click On mouse click.

4. Click the Effects tab to choose which animation effects you want.

Custom Animation

Animation order
1. Title

Timing | **Effects** | Chart Effects | Play Settings

Entry animation and sound
Fly From Left
[No Sound]

After animation
Don't Dim

Introduce text
All at once
☐ Grouped by 1st
   level paragraphs

☐ In reverse order
☑ Animate attached shape

OK | Cancel | Preview

- In the Entry animation and sound group, you can choose how an object appears, such as Fly from Left, Crawl from Right, Dissolve, or Wipe Down. You can also specify a sound to be played when the object enters the slide.

- In the After animation box, you can tell PowerPoint 97 what to do with the object after the animation: Hide the object, dim the object, change the object to a specified color, hide the object after you click the mouse, or do nothing.

- In the Introduce text grouping, you can set three methods for text to appear: all at once, by words, or by letters. If you want the animation for text objects to be applied in reverse order, allowing you to build slides from the bottom up, check the In reverse order check box. For text objects, you can have the animation apply separately to each paragraph, or you can group paragraphs based on their outline level by checking the Grouped by level paragraphs box and choosing a level in the drop-down list.

5. Repeat Steps 3 and 4 for any other objects you want to animate.

You can also add slide transition effects that are applied as each slide is displayed. For more information, see the procedure "Transitions," later in this part.

There are three other ways to apply basic animations to slide objects:

✦ The most popular animation settings can be applied by choosing Slide Show⇨Preset Animations.

✦ In Slide Sorter view, a drop-down list shows the most popular animation settings. Just click the slide you want to animate and choose the appropriate setting from the drop-down list.

✦ Choose View➪Toolbars➪Animation Effects to summon the Animation Effects toolbar, which contains buttons that apply several common animation effects with a single mouse click.

Clip Art

Here is the procedure for adding clip art from the Office 97 clip art collection to your presentation:

1. Move to the slide that you want to decorate with clip art. (If you want the clip art to appear on every slide, move to the master slide by choosing View➪Master➪Slide Master or by Shift-clicking the Slide View button.)

2. Choose Insert➪Picture➪Clip Art or click the Insert Clip Art button. The Clip Gallery dialog box pops up.

3. Select the category from the Clip Art list box that contains the picture you want.

When the Clip Gallery appears, the last category you used is selected. If you're using Clip Gallery for the first time, All Categories is selected; this category shows all the Clip pictures in your collection, allowing you to browse the gallery. To narrow your search, scroll the Clip Art list until you find the category that you want and click it.

4. Select the specific picture you want. Clip Gallery shows several pictures at a time, but you can see other pictures from the same category by scrolling through the pictures. When the picture you want comes into view, click it.

5. Click the Insert button to insert the picture.

PowerPoint 97 sticks the picture right in the middle of the slide, which is probably not where you want it. You can move it and resize it by dragging it with the mouse.

The first time you use Clip Gallery after installing PowerPoint 97, Clip Gallery realizes that it hasn't added the PowerPoint 97 clip art to the gallery, so it automatically adds the clip art. This process can take a while, so be prepared.

Notice that Clip Gallery has tabs for sounds and videos as well as clip art. You can use these tabs to add sounds and movies to your presentations, following the same procedure to select the clip you want to insert.

 If your computer has an Internet connection, you can click the Connect to Web button to connect to Microsoft's clip art page on the World Wide Web to obtain additional clip art pictures, sounds, and videos.

For more information, see Chapter 11 of *PowerPoint 97 For Windows For Dummies.*

Color Scheme

A presentation's *color scheme* is a set of coordinated colors that are used for various elements of the presentation's slides, such as the slide background, title text, body text, and so on. You can easily change a presentation's color scheme by following this procedure:

1. If you want to change the color scheme for an entire presenta-
tion, switch to Slide Master view by choosing View⇨Master⇨ Slide Master. To change the color scheme only for a specific slide, switch to Slide view by choosing View⇨Slide and go to the slide you want to change.

2. Choose Format⇨Slide Color Scheme to summon the Color Scheme dialog box.

3. Click the color scheme you'd like to use.

4. Click the Apply to All button.

To customize the color scheme, click the Custom tab and then choose whatever colors you would like to use for various slide elements.

Creating a New Presentation

The easiest way to create a new PowerPoint 97 presentation is to use the AutoContent Wizard. Here is the procedure:

1. Start PowerPoint 97 by clicking the Start button in the taskbar (usually found at the bottom-left of the screen). Choose Pro-grams⇨Microsoft PowerPoint. PowerPoint 97 comes to life and displays the following dialog box:

2. Click the AutoContent Wizard radio button and then click the OK button. The AutoContent Wizard comes to life.

3. Click the Next button. AutoContent Wizard asks what type of presentation you want to create.

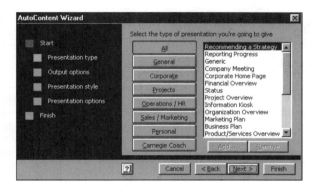

4. Select the presentation you want to create from the list box and then click the Next button. The Wizard politely asks how the presentation will be used.

5. Select whether you are creating a live presentation or an online presentation and then click the Next button. The Wizard asks what kind of output you want to create for the presentation.

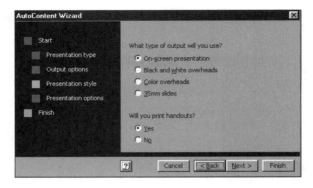

6. Select the output options you want and then click the Next button. The Wizard demands to know the presentation title, your name, and any other information you want to include on the presentation's first slide.

7. Type the requested information in the appropriate fields and then click the Next button. The Wizard displays its final screen.

8. Click the Finish button to create the presentation.

Hiding Background Objects

A *slide master* is a model slide layout that governs the appearance of all the slides in a presentation. PowerPoint 97 lets you add background objects to the slide master so that the objects appear on every slide in your presentation. For example, you can create a fancy logo or some other slick graphic effect to add spice to your slides.

Occasionally, though, you may want to create a slide or two that doesn't have these background objects. To do so, you must hide the background objects by following this procedure:

1. Display the slide you want to show with a plain background.

2. Choose Format⬗Background. The Background dialog box appears.

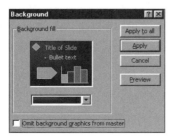

3. Check the Omit background graphics from master check box.

4. Click the Apply button or press Enter.

This procedure for hiding background objects applies only to the current slide or notes page. Other slides or notes pages are not affected.

You can hide background objects for all slides by calling up the Format⇨Background command, checking the Omit background graphics from master check box, and then clicking the Apply to all button.

If you want to remove some but not all of the background objects from a single slide, try this trick:

1. Follow the preceding procedure to hide background objects for the slide.

2. Call up the Slide Master by choosing View⇨Master⇨Slide Master.

3. Hold down the Shift key and click each object that you want to appear on the slide.

4. Press Ctrl+C to copy these objects to the Clipboard.

5. Return to Slide view by choosing View⇨Slide.

6. Press Ctrl+V to paste the objects from the Clipboard. The objects will be pasted at their original locations on the slide.

7. Choose Draw⇨Order⇨Send to Back from the Drawing toolbar if the background objects obscure other slide objects or text.

Keyboard Shortcuts

The following tables list the most useful keyboard shortcuts in PowerPoint 97.

Keyboard shortcuts for editing slides

Shortcut	What It Does
Ctrl+X	Cuts selected text to the Clipboard.
Ctrl+C	Copies selected text to the Clipboard.
Ctrl+V	Pastes the contents of the Clipboard.
Ctrl+Z	Undoes the last action.
Ctrl+Delete	Deletes from the insertion point to the end of the word.
Ctrl+Backspace	Deletes from the insertion point to the beginning of the word.

(continued)

Shortcut	What It Does
Ctrl+F	Calls up a dialog box to find text.
Ctrl+H	Calls up a dialog box to replace text.
Ctrl+M	Inserts a new slide by using the AutoLayout dialog box.
Ctrl+Shift+M	Inserts a new slide without using the AutoLayout dialog box.
Alt+Shift+D	Inserts the date on the Slide Master.
Alt+Shift+T	Inserts the time on the Slide Master.
Alt+Shift+P	Inserts the page number on the Slide Master.
Ctrl+D	Duplicates the selected objects.
Ctrl+ ←	Moves the insertion point one word to the left.
Ctrl+ →	Moves the insertion point one word to the right.
Ctrl+ ↑	Moves the insertion point to the preceding paragraph, except in Outline view, in which it moves to the preceding slide.
Ctrl+ ↓	Moves the insertion point to the next paragraph, except in Outline view, in which it moves to the next slide.
Ctrl+End	Moves the insertion point to the end of the page.
Ctrl+Home	Moves the insertion point to the top of the page.
Ctrl+Alt+PgUp	Moves to the preceding slide in Slide Sorter view.
Ctrl+Alt+PgDn	Moves to the next slide in Slide Sorter view.
Ctrl+A	Selects everything.

Keyboard shortcuts for formatting text

Shortcut	What It Does
Ctrl+B	Makes text **bold.**
Ctrl+I	Sets the font to *italic.*
Ctrl+U	Underlines text.
Ctrl+Shift+F	Activates the font control in the Formatting toolbar so you can change the font.
Ctrl+Shift+P	Activates the font size control on the Formatting toolbar so you can change the point size.
Ctrl+Shift+ >	Increases the point size to the next available size.
Ctrl+Shift+ <	Decreases the point size to the preceding size.
Ctrl+L	Left-aligns the paragraph.
Ctrl+R	Right-aligns the paragraph.
Ctrl+J	Justifies the paragraph.
Ctrl+E	Centers the paragraph.

Keyboard shortcuts for working with outlines

Shortcut	What It Does
Alt+Shift+ ←	Promotes the selected paragraphs.
Alt+Shift+ →	Demotes the selected paragraphs.
Alt+Shift+ ↑	Moves the selected paragraphs up.
Alt+Shift+ ↓	Moves the selected paragraphs down.
Alt+Shift+A	Shows all text and headings.
Alt+Shift+−	Collapses all text under a heading.
Alt+Shift+ +	Expands all text under a heading.
/ (on numeric keypad)	Hides or shows character formatting.

Notes

PowerPoint 97 enables you to create separate notes to accompany your slides to help you remember what you want to say. The beauty of notes is that the audience doesn't see them, so they think you are winging it when in fact you are relying on your notes. You can print notes pages which include a small image of the complete slide along with the notes for that slide. To add notes to a slide, follow this procedure:

1. In Slide or Outline view, move to the slide to which you want to add notes.

2. Switch to Notes Page view by clicking the Notes Page View button.

3. Adjust the zoom factor with the Zoom drop-down list on the Standard toolbar, if necessary, so you can read the notes text.

4. If necessary, scroll the display to bring the notes text into view. (The notes text appears beneath the slide image.)

5. Click in the notes area, where it reads Click to add text.

6. Type away.

The text you type appears in the notes area. You can use any of the PowerPoint 97 standard word processing features, such as cut, copy, and paste, as you create your notes. Press Enter to create new paragraphs.

After you switch to Notes Page view, you don't have to return to Slide view or Outline view to add notes for other slides. Use the scroll bar or the PgUp and PgDn keys to add notes for other slides.

For more information, see Chapter 18 of *PowerPoint 97 For Windows For Dummies.*

Publishing on the Web

PowerPoint 97 includes a new Wizard that saves your presentation in HTML format so it can be published on the Internet's World Wide Web. Each slide in your presentation is saved as a separate HTML file, and navigation buttons are automatically added so that the user can easily move from slide to slide.

To use the HTML Wizard, follow these steps:

1. Choose File⇨Save as HTML. The Save as HTML Wizard appears, as shown in the following figure:

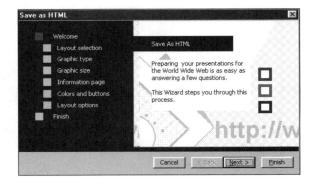

2. Click the Next button to get the Wizard started.

3. Answer each of the questions posed by the Wizard and then click the Next button to proceed to the next Wizard page.

The Wizard asks various questions about how you want your HTML document to be created. In each case, the Wizard provides a small preview area that shows how your choice will affect the final appearance of the document.

4. When you reach the last Wizard page, click the Finish button.

The Save as HTML Wizard saves your presentation as a series of HTML and graphic files in a separate folder created just for your presentation (one of the questions you must answer when running the Wizard is where you would like this folder to be created).

TIP

PowerPoint 97 comes with several templates that are designed specifically for online presentations that can be converted to HTML. One of the most popular of these templates is the Personal Home Page template. For more information, see the section "Creating a Presentation," earlier in this part.

Rearranging Slides

You can quickly rearrange slides by switching to Slide Sorter view, in which you can see a thumbnail version of each slide in a presentation. Here's the procedure:

 1. Switch to Slide Sorter view by clicking the Slide Sorter View button at the bottom-left corner of the screen or by choosing View⇨Slide Sorter. PowerPoint 97 switches to Slide Sorter view, as the following figure shows:

Slide Finder	? ✕

Find Presentation | List of Favorites

File:

Add to Favorites   Display   Browse...

Select Slides:

Insert   Insert All   Close

2. To move a slide, click and drag it to a new location. PowerPoint 97 adjusts the display to show the new arrangement of slides and automatically renumbers the slides.

3. To delete a slide, click the slide and press the Delete key or choose Edit⇨Delete Slide. (The Delete key works on an entire slide only in Slide Sorter view.)

4. To add a new slide, click the slide that you want the new slide to precede and then click the Insert New Slide button to summon the New Slide dialog box. Then click the slide layout you want to use and click the OK button to insert the slide. To edit the contents of the slide, return to Slide or Outline view.

If your presentation contains more slides than fit on-screen at the same time, you can use the scroll bars to scroll the display. Or you can change the zoom factor to make the slides smaller. Click the down arrow next to the zoom size, and select a smaller zoom percentage.

Recurring Text

To add recurring text to each slide, follow this procedure:

1. Call up the Slide Master, if it's not displayed already, by Shift-clicking the Slide View button.

2. Click the Text Box button on the Drawing toolbar.

3. Click where you want to add text.

4. Type the text that you want to appear on each slide.

5. Format the text however you want.

6. Click the Slide View button to return to Slide view.

To add a graphic that recurs on each slide, click the Insert ClipArt button on the Standard toolbar to insert any clip art picture supplied with PowerPoint 97 or choose Insert⇔Picture to insert a picture file.

To delete an object from the Slide Master, click it and press Delete. To delete a text object, you must first click the object and then click the object frame again. Then press Delete.

If the object won't select when you click it, you probably fell back into Slide view. Shift-click the Slide View button or choose View⇔Master⇔ Slide Master again to call up the Slide Master.

Slide Finder

PowerPoint 97 includes a new feature called *slide finder* that helps you quickly copy slides from other presentations into your presentation. Slide finder can search presentations that are stored on your hard disk or on presentations that are stored on other computers on a network. To use Slide Finder, follow these steps:

1. In Slide, Outline, or Slide Sorter view, move to the location where you would like to insert a slide stolen from another presentation.

2. Choose Insert⇔Slides from Files. The Slide Finder dialog box appears.

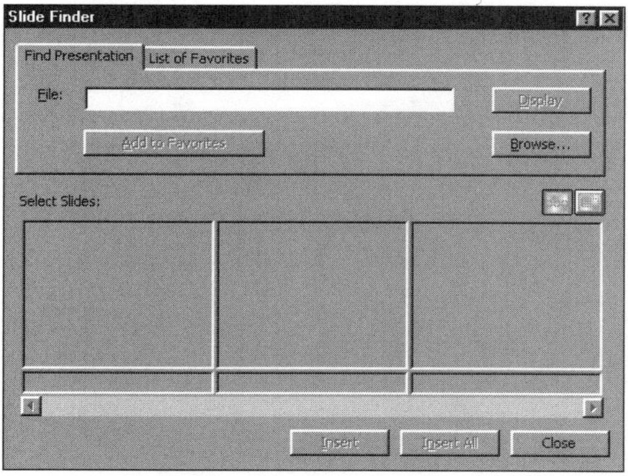

3. Click the Browse button to summon the Insert Slides from Files dialog box shown in the following figure:

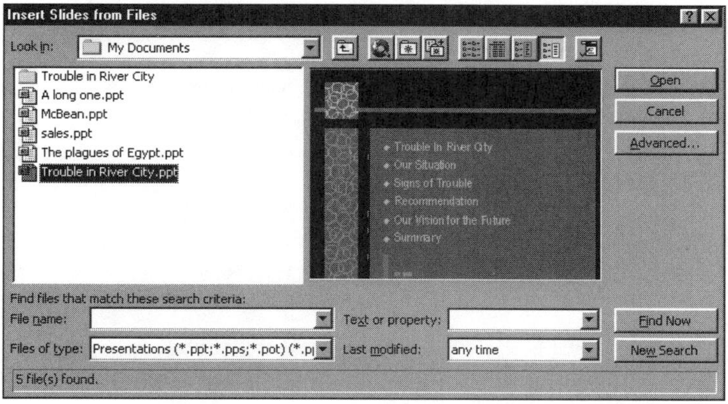

4. Locate the file you want to copy slides from and click the Open button to return to the Slide Finder dialog box.

If you want to locate a presentation file that contains a particular word or phrase, type the word or phrase in the Text or property field and then click the Find now button. PowerPoint 97 displays a list of the presentations which contain the word or phrase you typed.

5. Click the Display button. The Slide Finder dialog box displays the slides in the presentation.

6. Select the slide you want to insert. Use the scroll bar if necessary.

7. Click the Insert button.

8. Repeat Steps 6 and 7 if you want to copy additional slides from the presentation.

9. Click the Close button after you insert all the slides you need.

Summary Slide

You can quickly create a summary slide that contains the titles of some or all of the slides in your presentation by following these steps:

1. Switch to Outline or Slide Sorter View.

2. Select the slides you want to include in the summary. To summarize the entire presentation, press Ctrl+A to select all of the presentation's slides.

3. Click the Summary Slide button. PowerPoint 97 inserts the summary slide in front of the selected slides.

In Outline view, the Summary Slide button can be found in the Outline toolbar near the left edge of the screen. In Slide Sorter view, the Summary Slide button appears on the Slide Sorter toolbar which appears at the top of the screen, beneath the Formatting toolbar.

Templates

A *template* is a PowerPoint 97 presentation that is used as a model to create other presentations. When you create a new presentation using the AutoContent Wizard, the Wizard automatically selects a template for your presentation. As an alternative, you can select a template yourself when creating a presentation by choosing File➪New and selecting a template from the New Presentation dialog box that appears.

If at any time you decide that you don't like the appearance of your presentation, you can change the presentation's look without changing its contents by assigning a new template to the presentation. To do that, follow these steps:

1. Choose Format➪Apply Design. The Apply Design dialog box appears.

2. Click the template you want to use. The Preview area shows a preview of each template as you select it.

3. Click the Apply button.

Transitions

A transition is a visual effect that appears when a PowerPoint 97 slide show moves from one slide to the next. PowerPoint 97 lets you choose from among many different transition effects, and you can specify a different effect for each slide. In addition, you can easily add sound effects to add even more pizzazz to your presentations. To set the transitions between slides, follow this procedure:

1. Switch to Slide View or Slide Sorter view by choosing View⇨Slide or View⇨Slide Sorter.

2. Select the slide to which you want to add a transition. Note that the transition always occurs *before* the slide you select. So to set the transition to occur between the first and second slides, select the second slide.

3. Choose Slide Show⇨Slide Transition. The Slide Transition dialog box appears.

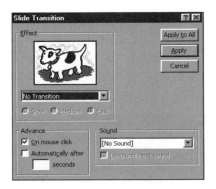

4. Select the transition effect you want from the Effect drop-down list box.

5. Select the speed of the transition by clicking the Slow, Medium, or Fast radio buttons. (Fast is almost always best.)

6. Choose a sound to accompany the transition from the Sound drop-down box.

7. If you want the slide show to run itself automatically, check the Automatically after check box and then enter the number of seconds you want the slide to be displayed. If you want to control the pace of the slide show, check the On mouse click check box.

8. Click the Apply button or press Enter.

For more information, see Chapter 16 of *PowerPoint 97 For Windows For Dummies.*

Viewer

You can transfer a PowerPoint 97 presentation to a diskette, from which you can run the presentation on any Windows 95 computer by using a special program called the PowerPoint 97 Viewer. The following sections present the procedures for using the Viewer.

Using the Pack and Go Wizard

To prepare a presentation for use with the PowerPoint 97 Viewer, use
the Pack and Go Wizard. Here's the procedure:

1. Open the presentation you want to copy to diskette.

2. Choose File⇨Pack and Go. The Pack and Go Wizard appears.

3. Click Next. The Wizard asks which presentation you want to
include.

4. Click Next. The Wizard asks whether you want to copy the
presentation to drive A or to a different drive.

5. Change the drive letter if necessary and then click Next. The Wizard now asks whether you want to Include Linked Files and Embed TrueType fonts. It's usually a good idea to check both options.

6. Click Next again. The Wizard asks whether you want to include the PowerPoint 97 Viewer.

It's best to include the Viewer, just in case the computer you want to run the presentation on doesn't have PowerPoint 97 installed.

7. Click Next. The Wizard's last screen appears.

8. Insert a diskette in the diskette drive.

9. Click the Finish button.

Copying a packed presentation onto another computer

You can't run a presentation directly from the disk created by the Pack and Go Wizard. Instead, you must first copy the presentation from the diskette to another computer's hard drive by following these steps:

1. Insert the diskette that contains the packed presentation into the disk drive on the computer from which you want to run the presentation.

2. Open the My Computer window by double-clicking its icon and then select the diskette drive into which you inserted the diskette.

3. Double-click the Pngsetup icon to run the Pack and Go Setup program.

4. Follow the instructions that appear on-screen.

Running a slide show by using the Viewer

After you copy the presentation to the other computer, you can run it with the Viewer by following this procedure:

1. Start PowerPoint 97 Viewer by double-clicking its icon in the folder into which you copied the presentation. The Viewer appears.

2. Select the presentation you want to show.

3. Click the Show button.

If you want to set up a computer to run a slide show over and over again all day, click the Loop continuously until 'Esc' check box.

Viewing Your Presentation

Here's the procedure for displaying a slide show:

1. Click the Slide Show View button. The first slide in your presentation appears.

2. To advance to the next slide, press Enter, press the spacebar, or click the left mouse button.

3. Press Esc to end the slide show.

During the slide show, you can use the following keyboard tricks:

To Do This	Press Any of These Keys
Display next slide	Enter, spacebar, right arrow, down arrow, PgDn, N
Display previous slide	Backspace, left arrow, up arrow, PgUp, P
Display first slide	1+Enter
Display specific slide	Slide number+Enter
Toggle screen black	B, period
Toggle screen white	W, comma
Show or hide pointer	A, = (equals)
Erase screen doodles	E
Stop or restart automatic show	S, + (plus)
Display next slide even if hidden	H
Display specific hidden slide	Slide number of hidden slide+Enter
Change pen to arrow	Ctrl+A
Change arrow to pen	Ctrl+P
End slide show	Esc, Ctrl+Break, – (minus)

To set up a presentation so that it runs continuously on the computer, choose Slide Show⇨Set up show to summon the Set Up Show dialog box. Check the Loop continuously until 'Esc' option and the Using timings, if present option and then click the OK button.

Part VI

Access 97

Access 97 is the powerful database program that comes with Microsoft Office 97 Professional. Because the Standard Edition of Office 97 does not include Access 97, you can skip this part if you don't have Office Professional.

Although Access 97 is a powerful database program that computer programmers use to create sophisticated applications, you don't need a Ph.D. in Computer Science to use Access 97. By using the information in this part, you can create simple databases, design custom forms and reports, and query your database to extract important information. For more information about Access 97, pick up a copy of *Access 97 For Windows For Dummies,* by John Kaufeld, published by IDG Books Worldwide, Inc.

In this part . . .

- ✔ **Adding a field to an existing table**
- ✔ **Creating a new database**
- ✔ **Creating a query**
- ✔ **Creating a report**
- ✔ **Entering and editing data**
- ✔ **Using the Form Wizard**
- ✔ **Printing mailing labels**
- ✔ **Publishing database information on the World Wide Web**

Adding a Field to an Existing Table

After you create a database, adding additional fields to any of its tables is a simple matter. Follow these steps to create a new field by using a field in one of the sample tables as a model:

1. If the database's Switchboard is open, close the window by clicking its Close button (located in the upper-right corner, marked by an *X*) and then open the minimized Database window, as shown in the following figure. (The *Switchboard* is a menu that lets you access common database functions such as entering data or printing reports. The databases created by the Access 97 database templates all include switchboards.)

2. If the Tables tab is not selected, click the tab to access its options; then click the table to which you want to add a field and click the Design button. The Table window appears, as shown in the following figure:

3. Click the row in which you want to insert the new field.

To insert the new field after the existing fields, click the first blank row.

4. Click the Build button in the toolbar.

The Field Builder dialog box appears, as shown in the following figure:

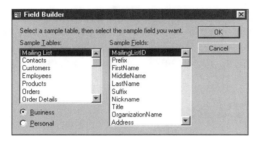

5. Select from the Sample Tables list the sample table that contains the field you want to add and then select the field from the Sample Fields list.

6. Click the OK button.

Access 97 adds the field to the table and closes the dialog box.

7. Click the Close button in the upper-right corner of the table design window.

Access 97 asks whether you want to save changes to the table design; click the Yes button.

If you prefer to define the field manually or if no similar field exists in any of the sample databases, skip Steps 4 through 6. Instead, follow Steps 1 through 3 of the preceding set of steps and then follow these steps:

1. From the Database window, click the Tables tab, click the table to which you want to add a field, and then click the Design button.

The Table window appears.

2. To insert the new field after the existing fields, click the first blank row.

To insert the new field among the existing fields, click where you want to insert the new field and then click the Insert Row button in the toolbar.

3. Type the name of the new field in the Field Name column.

4. Select the field type from the drop-down list in the Data Type column.

(The down arrow that activates the drop-down list appears after you move the insertion point to the Data Type column. Click the arrow to display the list of field types.)

5. Adjust the properties for the field as necessary, using the properties list that appears at the bottom of the Table window. To change one of the property settings, click the property and type a new value.

6. Click the close button in the upper-right corner of the Table window to dismiss the window.

After Access 97 asks whether you want to save changes to the table design, click the Yes button.

Creating a New Database

Creating a database from scratch can be a tedious chore, best left to database experts. Access 97, however, comes with a friendly Database Wizard that can perform most of the dirty work for you. All you need to do is answer a few simple questions and enjoy a cup of coffee while the Wizard creates your database fields, forms, and reports. Just follow these steps:

1. Click the Database Wizard option button in the dialog box that appears right after you start Access 97 and then click the OK button. The New dialog box appears.

If you already have another database open, close that database by choosing File⇨Close and then choose File⇨New or click the New button to open the New dialog box.

2. Click the Databases tab of the New dialog box to reveal the list of Database templates, as shown in the following figure:

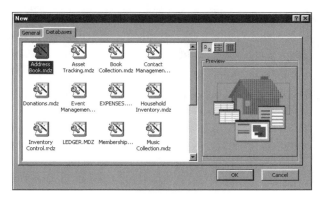

3. Click in the list the database template that best represents the type of database you want to create.

4. Click the OK button.

The File New Database dialog box appears, as shown in the following figure:

5. Type a name for your database in the File Name text box or leave the name that Access 97 proposes if that name is satisfactory.

6. Click the Create button.

Access 97 whirs and spins for a moment and then displays the first screen of the Database Wizard, as shown in the following figure:

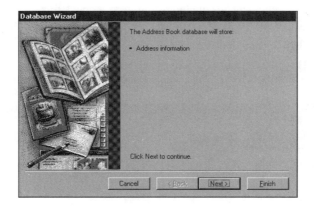

7. Click the Next button to start the Wizard.

The Wizard proposes certain fields to be included in the database but allows you to select which ones should actually be included, as shown in the following figure:

8. Scan the Fields in the table list, adding or removing fields from the list of fields proposed for each table by clicking the check box next to the field name.

Note: If the database has more than one table, select the table that you want to examine in the Tables in the database list box.

9. If you want the Wizard to place some sample data in the database, click the Yes, include sample data check box.

10. After you're satisfied with the arrangement of fields for the table, click the Next button.

The Wizard then asks what style you want it to use for dialog boxes used by the database, as shown in the following figure:

11. Select from the list the display style that suits your fancy and then click the <u>N</u>ext button.

The Wizard now asks for your report style preference, which affects such things as the typeface and background colors for your reports, as shown in the following figure:

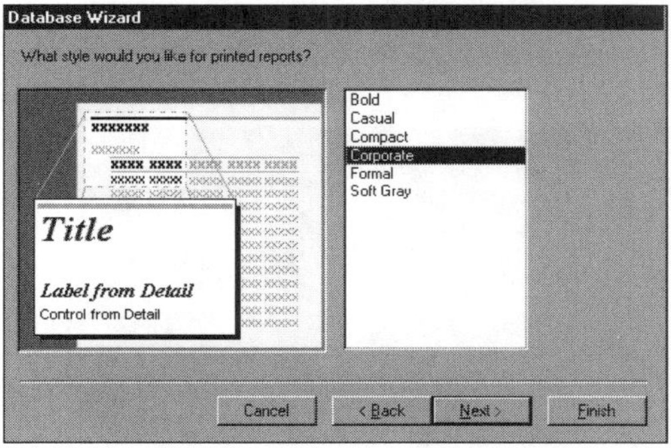

12. Select from the list the report style that pleases you and then click the <u>N</u>ext button.

The Wizard asks a few more annoying questions, including what you want to name your database.

13. Type a title for the database in the text box if you are not satisfied with the Wizard's proposed title.

14. If you want to include a picture in all the reports for the database, check the Yes, I'd like to include a picture check box and then click the Picture button and select a picture for the reports.

15. Click the <u>N</u>ext button.

The Wizard displays its final screen, as shown in the following figure:

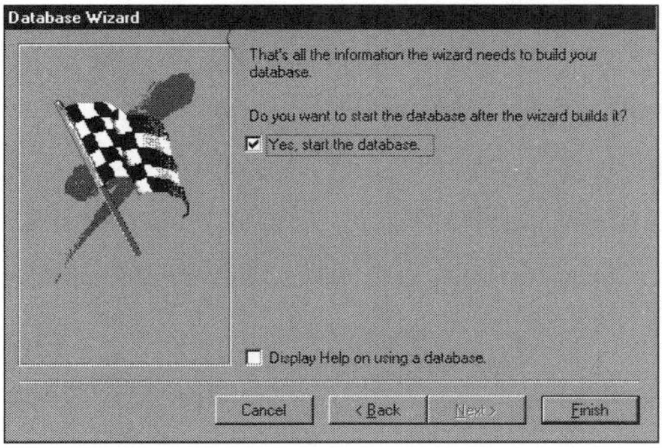

16. Click the Finish button.

Be patient while the Wizard creates the database tables, forms, and reports. After the Wizard finishes, Access 97 opens the database.

Notice that the Database Wizard creates a *Switchboard,* which is a menu that's customized for each type of database. The following figure shows the Switchboard for the Address Book database.

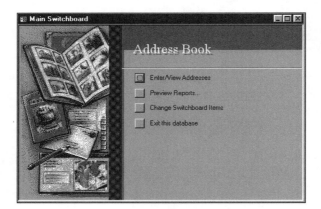

To use the Switchboard, just click the buttons that appear next to each option.

To dismiss the Switchboard, click the Switchboard's close button in the upper-right corner. Then you can open the minimized database window for that database and use the Access 97 database functions directly.

Creating a Query

A query is the most powerful and difficult-to-use feature of Access 97. Before you create a query, you need to know the following details:

✦ Which tables are involved in the query

✦ Which fields you want the query result to show

✦ The sequence into which you want the query result sorted

✦ Which criteria you want to apply to determine which records Access 97 selects

Here's the blow-by-blow procedure for creating a query:

1. Open the database for which you want to create a query by choosing File⇨Open. Then click the Queries tab in the Database window and click the New button.

The New Query dialog box appears, as shown in the following figure:

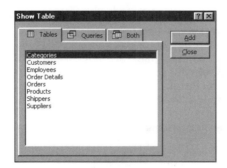

2. Select Design View from the list and then click the OK button.

You switch to Query Design view. When Query Design view first appears, a Query window in which you construct your query is partially overlaid by a Show Tables dialog box, which you use to select the table or tables to be used for the query.

(If you prefer, you can select one of the query design wizards. If you do, skip the rest of these steps and instead follow the instructions that the wizard offers.)

3. Double-click each table that you want to include in the query and then click the Close button after you finish adding to the query all the tables you need. This dismisses the Show Table dialog box to provide direct access to the Query window.

4. Double-click each field in the table that was added to the query window that you want to include in the query. Approach 97 adds a field to a column in the bottom part of the query window.

If you want the records selected by the query to be sorted, select the sort fields first. You can specify that any or all of the fields included in the query be used as sort fields, but the sort fields must appear in the field section at the bottom of the query window in the order in which you want them to be used for sorting. For example, if you want records to be sorted first by Region and then by City, you must select the Region field prior to the City field for the query.

The following figure shows what the query window looks like after you select several fields:

5. Select the sort order for the query result.

You select the sort order by first clicking the Sort row for each field by which you want to sort the result. Then, to reveal the list of sort choices, click the drop-down arrow that appears and select Ascending or Descending sort sequence from the list. Follow this procedure for each field by which you want to sort the query result. In the example shown in the following figure, the query result sorts first by region and then by city:

6. Type the query selection criteria in the Criteria rows for the fields with values you want to test.

In the example shown in the following figure, Access 97 tests the Region field so that the query result includes only those records in which the Region field is "OR" or "WA." (Access 97 automatically adds the quotation marks when you type the criteria.)

In the Criteria row you can use any of the symbols shown in the following table for more precise control over which records Access 97 selects.

Symbol	Meaning
=	Equal to
<	Less than
>	Greater than
<=	Less than or equal to
>=	Greater than or equal to
<>	Not equal to

You can also specify a range of values by typing **Between . . . and**, as in **Between 10 and 50**. Or, you can use Like if you are unsure of the spelling.

7. Click the Run button on the toolbar to run the query.

The query results appear in a separate window, as shown in the following figure:

Region	City	Company Name	Contact Name
OR	Elgin	Hungry Coyote Import Store	Yoshi Latimer
OR	Eugene	Great Lakes Food Market	Howard Snyder
OR	Portland	The Big Cheese	Liz Nixon
OR	Portland	Lonesome Pine Restaurant	Fran Wilson
WA	Kirkland	Trail's Head Gourmet Provisioners	Helvetius Nagy
WA	Seattle	White Clover Markets	Karl Jablonski
WA	Walla Walla	Lazy K Kountry Store	John Steel

Record: 1 of 7

8. If the query doesn't work as you expected, close the query result by clicking its close button in the upper-right corner of the query result window and then work on the query setting to correct the problem.

If the query works as expected, choose File⇨Save from the main Access menu bar to save the query.

The Save As dialog box appears, as shown in the following figure:

Save As

Query Name:
OR/WA Customers

OK
Cancel

9. Type a meaningful name for the query in the Query Name text box and then click the OK button.

After you save the query, you can run that query at any time by opening the Database window, clicking the Queries tab, and double-clicking the query name in the list of queries. Or, you can just click the query name once and click the Open button.

For more information, see Chapter 11 of *Access 97 For Windows For Dummies*.

Creating a Report

Creating a report in Access 97 is easy if you use the Report Wizards. Report Wizards create various types of reports after asking you questions about the information you want to include. The following procedure shows how to create a simple tabular report, which prints a simple listing of database records with one record per line and the fields neatly lined up in columns. The procedure for creating other types of reports is similar.

Here is the procedure for creating a tabular report:

1. Choose File⇨Open to open the database for which you want to create a report, click the Reports tab in the Database window, and then click the New button.

The New Report dialog box appears, as shown in the following figure:

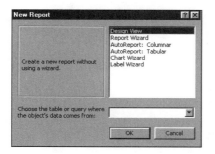

2. Select Report Wizard from the list of report types and then click the OK button.

The Report Wizard appears, as shown in the following figure:

3. Select the fields that you want to include in the report.

To select fields for the report, first select from the Tables/Queries drop-down list the table that contains the fields you want in the report. Then click in the Available Fields list the field that you want to include and click the > button. Access 97 removes the field you select from the Available Fields list and inserts that field

in the Selected Fields list. Repeat this step for each field that you want to include. In the following figure, I select three fields to include in the report:

4. After you select all the fields that you want to include, click the Next button.

The Report Wizard dialog box asks its next question, as shown in the following figure:

5. If you want to group the report by any of the fields, double-click the fields you want to use for grouping and then click the Next button.

The Wizard next asks about the sort order for the report.

6. Select from the first drop-down list the first field by which you want to sort the report.

The Report Wizard enables you to sort the report by up to four fields, and each field can be used to sort the report in ascending or descending sequence. In the following figure, I tell the Wizard to sort the report in CompanyName sequence:

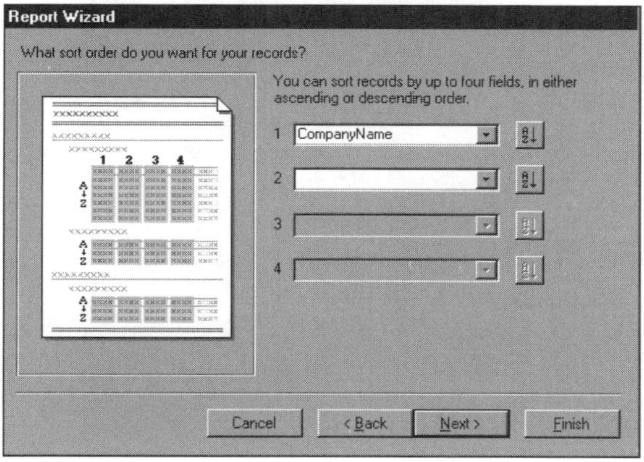

7. After you select the sorting sequence, click the Next button.

The Report Wizard dialog box asks some questions about the report layout, as shown in the following figure:

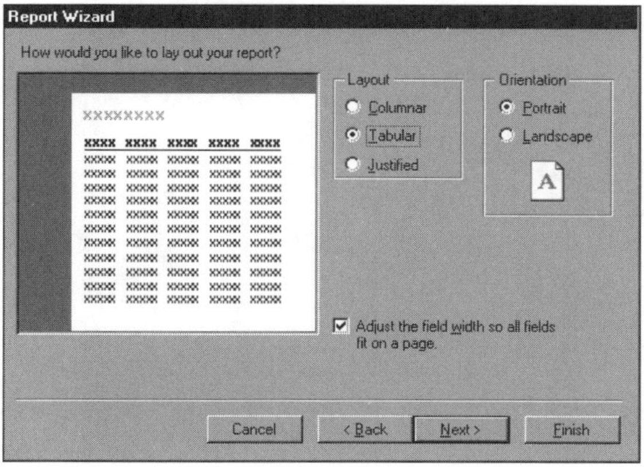

8. Select the layout options you want and then click the Next button.

You can select Columnar, Tabular, or Justified layout; Portrait or Landscape orientation; and whether you want the field widths adjusted automatically so that all fit on the page.

The Wizard then asks you what style to use for the report, as shown in the following figure:

9. Select from the list the report style that suits your fancy and then click the Next button.

The Report Wizard dialog box asks its final question, as shown in the following figure:

10. Change the report title in the text box if you don't like the one that the Wizard proposes and then click the Finish button.

The Wizard grinds and churns for a few moments while creating the report, and then the Wizard displays the report in preview mode, as shown in the following figure:

11. To print the report, click the Print button in the toolbar.

12. To save your report design, choose File⇨Save or click the Save button in the toolbar.

Entering and Editing Data

After you create a database, you can enter data into it. The exact procedures you must follow vary depending on the database, but here is a general procedure you can use:

1. From the main switchboard for the database, select one of the options that allows you to enter data. For example, the following figure shows the main switchboard for a Membership database. The first two items on this switchboard let you enter data.

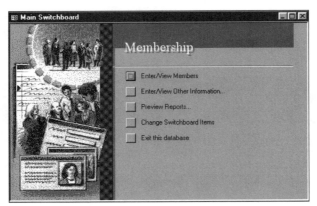

Selecting the first option on this switchboard brings up the following data entry form:

2. Type the information for each field, using the tab key to move from field to field.

3. When you have entered all of the information for one record, click the New Record button to create the record. You can then enter data for another record.

4. After you finish entering data, click the form's close button (the X in the top-right corner) to dismiss the form.

You can change data in an existing record by using one of the navigation buttons which appear at the bottom of the form to display the record. Then, use the tab key to move to the field you want to change, type a new value into the field, and press Enter. The navigation buttons are described in the following table:

Navigation Button	What It Does
⏮	Displays the first record in the database.
◀	Goes back one record.
▶	Goes forward one record.
⏭	Displays the last record in the database.

To delete a record, use the navigation buttons to call up the record you want to delete and then choose Edit⇨Delete Record. The following dialog box appears:

Click the Yes button to delete the record.

Publishing Database Information on the Web

One of the most talked-about new features of Access 97 is the Publish to the Web Wizard, which enables you to convert database objects to HTML files that you publish on the World Wide Web. To use the Publish to the Web Wizard, follow these steps:

1. Choose File⇨Open to open the database that you want to publish on the Web.

2. Choose File⇨Save to HTML/Web Formats⇨Publish to the Web. This action opens the Publish to the Web Wizard, as shown in the following figure:

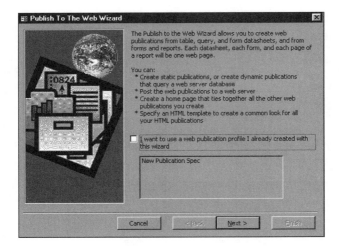

3. Click the Next button to start the Web Wizard. The next Publish to the Web Wizard dialog box appears, as shown in the following figure:

4. Select the database objects for which you want to create Web pages. You can select any of the database's tables, queries, forms, or reports by clicking the appropriate tab and selecting from the list the objects you want to include on the Web page.

5. After you select all the objects you want for the Web page, click the Next button. The dialog box shown in the following figure appears:

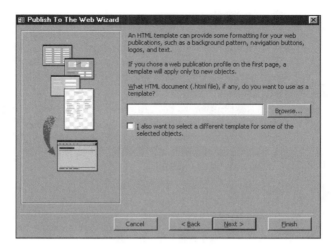

6. If you (or someone else) previously created an HTML file that you can use as a template for your database Web pages, type the name of that file into the text box or click the B̲rowse button to locate the file.

7. Click the N̲ext button to display the next dialog box, as shown in the following figure:

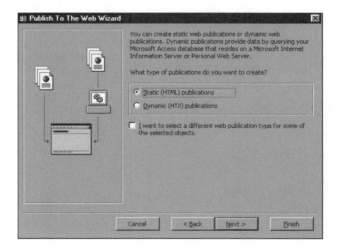

8. Choose whether you want the Web pages to be static or dynamic by selecting the appropriate radio button.

If you select Static (HTML) publications, Access 97 builds the pages from information available at the time you run the Publish to the Web Wizard. If you select Dynamic (HTML) publications, the HTML document created by the Wizard will query the database each time a user accesses the Web pages, so the user always sees up-to-date data.

_9._ Click the Next button to continue. The version of the dialog box shown in the following figure appears:

_10._ Type the location where you want the Web pages stored in the text box or click the Browse button to find the location. Then click the Next button to display the dialog box shown in the following figure:

11. Use the check box to specify whether you want to create a home page containing links to the pages you created for the database and change the filename if you don't want to use "default.htm" as the filename for your home page. Then click the Next button to continue to the next dialog box, as shown in the following figure:

12. Click the Finish button to create the Web pages.

Grab a cup of coffee while Access 97 creates the Web pages. Depending on the size of the database and the complexity of the objects you're converting to HTML format, this procedure may take a while.

Using the Form Wizard

One of the best features of Access 97 is that the program enables you to create custom-designed forms to enter data into or retrieve data from your database. You could spend hours creating forms from scratch. Or you can create a basic form in minutes by using the Form Wizard. To use the Wizard, just follow these steps:

1. Choose File➪Open to open the database for which you want to create a form, click the Forms tab in the Database window, and then click the New button. The New Form dialog box appears, as shown in the following figure:

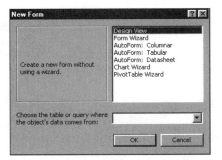

2. Select Form Wizard from the list of form types and select a table or query from the drop-down list. Then click the OK button. The Form Wizard appears, as shown in the following figure:

3. Select the fields that you want to include on the form. To select the fields, first select from the Tables/Queries list the table that contains the field you want to include on the form. Then click in the Available Field list the field that you want to include and click the > button. Access 97 removes the field you select from the Available Fields list and inserts the field in the Selected Fields list. Repeat this step for each field you want to include.

4. After you select all the fields that you want to include, click the Next button. The Form Wizard dialog box asks how you want the fields arranged on the form, as shown in the following figure:

Form Wizard

What layout would you like for your form?

- ⊙ **C**olumnar
- ○ **T**abular
- ○ **D**atasheet
- ○ **J**ustified

Cancel   < **B**ack   **N**ext >   **F**inish

5. Select the radio button for the field layout that you want.

You have the following four choices of form layouts:

- **Columnar:** The fields are arranged in a column, with one record shown on each form.

- **Tabular:** The fields are arranged in a tabular form, with one row of fields for each record. This format displays more than one record at a time.

- **Datasheet:** This layout arranges fields in a spreadsheetlike configuration. This layout also shows more than one record at a time.

- **Justified:** This layout arranges fields in a grid configuration, adjusting the width of each field so that the table aligns on both the left and right sides. If possible, the Form Wizard places more than one field in each row of the grid. In this layout, only one record is visible at a time.

6. Click the **N**ext button. The Form Wizard asks which form style you prefer. These styles provide different background images and text styles.

Form Wizard

What style would you like?

XXX
XXX
XXXX

Label Data

Clouds
Colorful 1
Colorful 2
Dusk
Evergreen
Flax
International
Pattern
Standard
Stone

Cancel   < Back   Next >   Finish

7. Select from the list the style that you prefer and then click the Next button. The Form Wizard displays its final screen, as shown in the following figure:

Form Wizard

What title do you want for your form?

Addresses1

That's all the information the wizard needs to create your form.

Do you want to open the form or modify the form's design?

● Open the form to view or enter information.
○ Modify the form's design.

☐ Display Help on working with the form?

Cancel   < Back   Next >   Finish

8. Type a title for the form in the text box and then click the Finish button. The Wizard creates and then displays the form, as shown in the following figure:

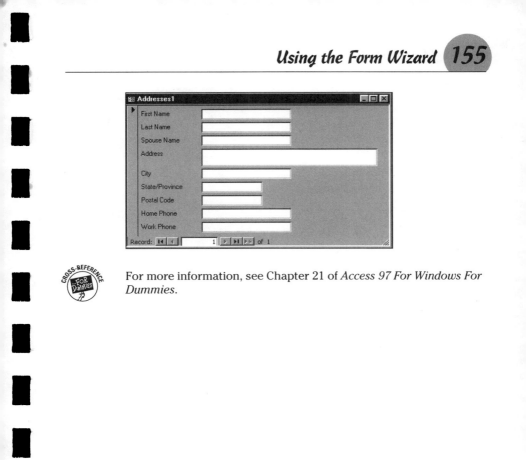

For more information, see Chapter 21 of *Access 97 For Windows For Dummies*.

Part VII

Outlook

This part covers Outlook, the new all-in-one personal information manager that comes with Microsoft Office 97. Outlook is similar to Schedule+, an address book and calendar program that came with older versions of Microsoft Office. Outlook includes all the features of Schedule+, plus it can even double as your e-mail program. For more information about Outlook, pick up a copy of *Microsoft Outlook For Dummies,* by Bill Dyszel, published by IDG Books Worldwide, Inc.

In this part . . .

✔ **Tracking appointments and events**

✔ **Creating and maintaining a contact list**

✔ **Sending and receiving e-mail**

✔ **Task management**

Calendar

 One of the main functions of Outlook is keeping a calendar so that you can track appointments and upcoming events. To switch to the Outlook calendar, click the Calendar icon in the Outlook Bar (the Outlook Bar is the list of icons along the left edge of the Outlook window) or choose Go⇨Calendar. The following figure shows what Outlook's calendar looks like:

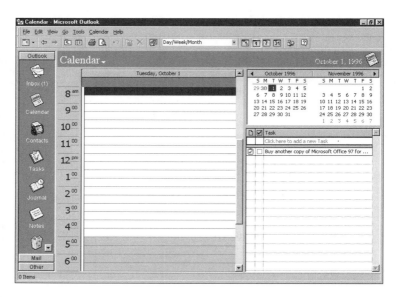

The following sections describe the most common procedures for using the Outlook calendar.

Canceling an appointment

To cancel an appointment, follow these steps:

1. Click the appointment in the calendar you want to cancel to select that appointment.

2. Click the Delete button. The appointment disappears from the calendar.

Changing views

Outlook gives you three calendar views: Day, Week, and Month. To change views, click the following buttons in the toolbar:

♦ Day

♦ Week

♦ Month

The Outlook calendar also enables you to view active appointments, scheduled events, annual events, and recurring appointments. You can see these views via the Current View drop-down list on the Standard toolbar.

Rescheduling an appointment

Here's the procedure for rescheduling an appointment by dragging it to a new time or date:

1. Switch to a calendar view that shows both the appointment you want to reschedule and the date to which you want to reschedule the appointment. (See the section "Changing Views" for more information.)

To move an appointment to a different time on the same day, for example, switch to Day view. To reschedule to a different day in the same week, switch to Week view.

2. Click the appointment to select it.

3. Drag the appointment to the new time and/or day.

You can also reschedule an appointment by double-clicking the appointment to open the Appointment dialog box and then adjusting the Start time and End time fields in the dialog box. (If you change the start time, the end time is automatically adjusted to keep the appointment the same length. If you change the end time, the start time is not changed. Instead, the duration of the appointment increases.)

Scheduling an appointment

To create an appointment, follow these steps:

1. Switch to the calendar view in which you prefer to work. Daily or weekly views are best for scheduling appointments. (See the section "Changing Views" for more information.)

2. Click the day on which you want to schedule the appointment.

3. Click the time slot during which you want to schedule the appointment.

   If you want the appointment to stretch beyond a single time interval, drag the mouse across the desired time periods.

4. Type a description for the appointment.

   You're done. The following figure shows a lunch appointment scheduled, shown in Day view:

Scheduling an event

An *event* is an item that occurs on a specific calendar date but does not have a particular time associated with it. Examples of events include birthdays, anniversaries, vacations, and so on.

To add an event to your calendar, follow these steps:

1. Switch to the calendar view in which you want to work — Day, Week, or Month. (See the section "Changing Views" for details.)

2. In the calendar, click the date on which the event occurs.

3. Choose Calendar⇨New Event from the Outlook menu bar.

   The Event dialog box appears, as shown in the following figure:

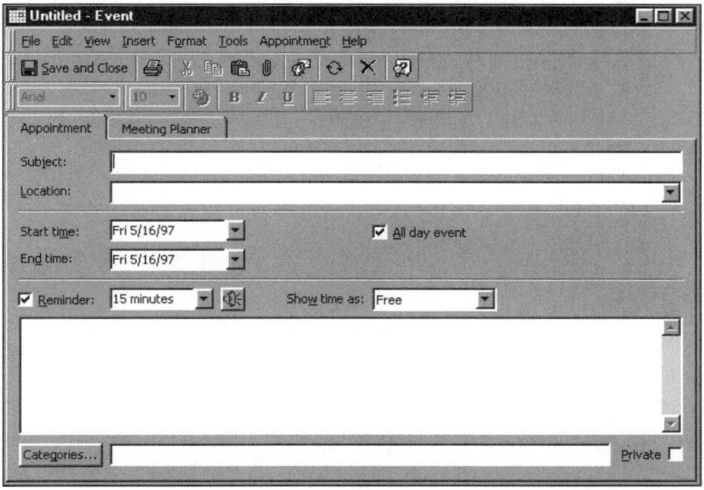

4. Type a description for the event in the Subject box.

5. If the event continues for more than one day, change the ending date by selecting a date from the End time drop-down list.

6. Click the Save and Close button.

The event appears on your calendar.

The following figure shows how a typical event appears in monthly calendar view:

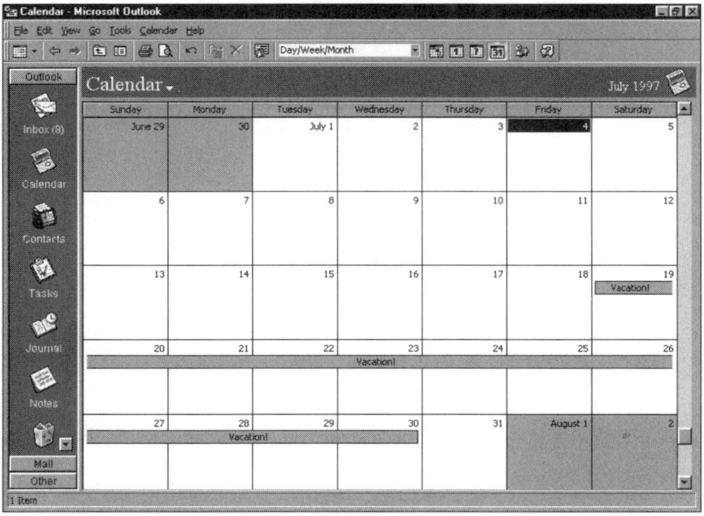

Scheduling a meeting

If everyone in your office uses Outlook and your computers are connected via a network, you can use the Plan a Meeting feature to schedule meetings electronically. Outlook automatically picks a time slot that's available for each participant and notifies everyone of the time and place of the meeting.

Follow these steps to plan a meeting:

1. Choose Calendar⇨Plan a Meeting. The Plan a Meeting dialog box appears, as shown in the following figure:

Plan a Meeting	_ □ ×

Wednesday, September 25, 1996

| | 4:00 | 9:00 10:00 11:00 12:00 1:00 2:00 3:0 |

All Attendees
✉ Doug Lowe
Type attendee name here

Invite Others...   □ Tentative ■ Busy ■ Out of Office

Meeting start time: Fri 9/27/96 ▼ 12:30 PM ▼   << AutoPick >>
Meeting end time: Fri 9/27/96 ▼ 1:00 PM ▼

Make Meeting   Close

2. Type the names of the people with whom you want to schedule a meeting in the All Attendees column. Or click the Invite Others button to summon the Select Attendees and Resources dialog box. This dialog box lets you select names from your address book. After you select everyone you want to invite, click the OK button to dismiss the Select Attendees and Resources dialog box.

Outlook retrieves each person's schedule so that you can see who has free time (and when).

3. Pick a time when everyone is free by clicking on the time in the schedule area of the Appointment dialog box. Or click AutoPick to have Outlook pick the time for you.

4. Click the Make Meeting button. Outlook displays the following window:

5. Type a subject for the meeting invitation in the Subjec_t box and a
location in the _Location box.

6. Click the _Send button in the window's toolbar to send the
invitations.

If someone invites you to a meeting, you receive an e-mail message
that includes three buttons you can click to reply to the invitation:
Accept, Decline, or Tentative. Click the appropriate button to reply to
the invitation.

Scheduling a recurring appointment

You can use Outlook to schedule recurring appointments, such as
staff meetings or other annoying appointments that you hate to go to
every day, week, or month. Here's the procedure:

1. Follow the procedure outlined in the section "Scheduling an
Appointment," earlier in this part, to create an appointment for
the next occurrence of the recurring date.

If you have a staff meeting from 12:00 to 1:30 every Friday
afternoon, for example, schedule the appointment for next Friday.

2. Double-click the appointment to open the Appointment window,
as shown in the following figure:

Friday Staff Meeting - Appointment

File Edit View Insert Format Tools Appointment Help

Save and Close | 🖨 | ✂ 📋 📋 📎 | 🔁 ↻ ✕ | 🗐

| Appointment | Meeting Planner |

Subject: | Friday Staff Meeting

Location: |

Start time: | Fri 9/27/96 | 12:00 PM | ☐ All day event
End time: | Fri 9/27/96 | 1:30 PM

☑ Reminder: | 15 minutes | 🔔 | Show time as: | Busy

Categories... | | Private ☐

🔁 **3.** Click the Recurrence button to open the Appointment Recurrence dialog box, as shown in the following figure:

Appointment Recurrence

Appointment time
Start: | 12:00 PM | End: | 1:30 PM | Duration: | 1.5 hours

Recurrence pattern
○ Daily   Recur every 1 week(s) on:
● Weekly   ☐ Sunday   ☐ Monday   ☐ Tuesday   ☐ Wednesday
○ Monthly   ☐ Thursday ☑ Friday   ☐ Saturday
○ Yearly

Range of recurrence
Start: | Fri 9/27/1996 | ● No end date
                           ○ End after: 10 occurrences
                           ○ End by: Fri 11/29/1996

OK | Cancel | Remove Recurrence

Outlook initially assumes that the appointment occurs every week on the same day and time. If this is not the case (for example, if the appointment should be every other week or monthly), you can make any necessary changes now.

4. If necessary, change the Recurrence pattern options to indicate the frequency of the appointment (Daily, Weekly, Monthly, or Yearly).

After you change the frequency option, a new set of controls appears in the Recurrence Pattern area of the Appointment Recurrence dialog box, enabling you to specify the exact schedule for the recurring appointment. To schedule an appointment that occurs only on the fourth Friday of every month, for example, you click Monthly. A set of list box controls then appears. These controls enable you to specify that the appointment occurs on a certain day of each month — in this case, on the fourth Friday.

5. Click the OK button and then click the Save and Close button.

 Outlook adds a special icon to the appointment in the calendar to indicate that the appointment is recurring.

Contacts

 Outlook also keeps an address book, which the program refers to as a *list of contacts*. To work with contacts, click the Contacts icon or choose Go⇨Contacts. Here is how Outlook appears when you call up your contacts:

Contacts - Microsoft Outlook			
File Edit View Go Tools Contacts Help			
Address Cards			
Contacts			*We - Win
Welcome to Contacts!	Duck, Daffey	Picard, Jean Luke	123
Adams, Gomez	Fife, Barney	Pierce, Benjamin F.	a
Adams, Grandmama	Flintstone, Fred	Potter, Sherman T.	b
Adams, Morticia	Hill, Harold	Presley, Elvis	c
Adams, Pugsley	Hullanan, Margaret	Pyle, Gomer	d
Adams, Wednesday	Hunnicut, B. J.	Pyle, Goober	e f
Balboa, Rocky	Jetson, George	Riker, William	g
Bird, Tweety	Kirk, James T.	Rubble, Barny	h
Blake, William	Klinger, Maxwell	Sarek	ij
Bunny, Buggs	LaForge, Jordie	Scott, Montgomery	k l
Burns, Frank	Lowe, Doug	Skywalker, Luke	m
Cat, Sylverster	Macentire, John	Solo, Han	n
Chapel, Christine	Malone, Sam	Spock	o
Checkov, Pavel	McCoy, Leonard	Sulu, Ikara	pq
Claven, Cliff	Mulcahey, Francis	Taylor, Andy	r s
Crane, Frazier	O'Rielly, Walter	Urkel, Steven Q.	t
Drevin, Frank	Petersen, Norm	Winchester, Charles Emmerson	uv wx yz
Mail			
Other			
51 Items			

You can use the following procedures to maintain your contact list.

Adding a contact

To add a contact to the Outlook address book, follow these steps:

1. Click the Insert New Contact button in the toolbar.

The Contact window appears, as in the following figure:

2. Fill in the blanks to record the contact's name, address, company, phone number, and other information. Use the tab key to jump from field to field. If the contact has an e-mail address, enter that address in the text box that appears next to the e-mail drop-down list near the bottom of the contact window.

Outlook performs a similar breakdown of the address you type in the Address text box to determine the street address, city, state, and zip code.

3. Click the All Fields tab if you want to record information not shown on the General tab.

For example, you can record the contact's birthday or anniversary in specific text boxes on the All Fields tab.

4. Click the Save and Close button.

Deleting a contact

To delete a contact from the Outlook address book, follow these steps:

1. Switch to Contacts view by choosing Go⊅Contacts. Then click the contact that you want to delete.

 2. Click the Delete button.

Updating a contact

If the address information or any other information for a contact changes, you can update the contact by following these steps:

1. Switch to Contacts view by choosing Go⊅Contacts. Then double-click the contact you want to change to open the Contact window.

2. Enter any changes in the fields on the Contact dialog box.

3. Click the Close button (the button with the X in the upper-right corner) to close the Contact dialog box.

4. After the program asks, click the Yes button to save your changes.

E-Mail

Outlook includes an integrated e-mail feature that can send and receive electronic mail from your various e-mail services. If you receive e-mail from your local area network, from the Internet, or from the Microsoft Network, Outlook can read e-mail from all three sources. That way, you don't need to fuss around with three separate e-mail programs.

To access the Outlook e-mail feature, click the Inbox icon or choose Go⊅Inbox. The following figure shows the Inbox:

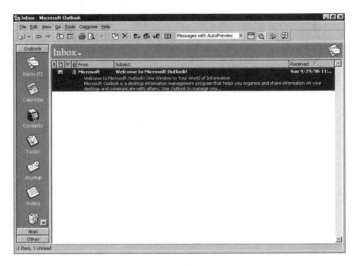

The following sections describe how to accomplish the most important tasks in using Outlook e-mail.

Reading e-mail

Reading e-mail is easy in Outlook. All you do is double-click the message you want to read in the Inbox. The message appears in its own window, as shown in the following figure:

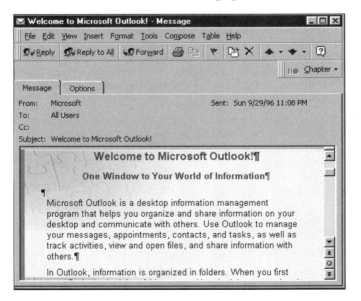

After you finish reading the message, close the window by clicking the Close button (the button with the X in the upper-right corner of the window). Or click any of the following buttons described in the following list to respond to the message or to read other messages:

- ◆ Displays the previous message in the Inbox.
- ◆ Displays the next message in the Inbox.
- ◆ Reply to the message.
- ◆ Save the message.
- ◆ Delete the message.
- ◆ Forward the message to another user.

Replying to e-mail

To reply to an e-mail message, follow these steps:

1. Click the Reply button to open the window shown in the following figure:

```
RE: Welcome to Microsoft Outlook! - Message                    _ □ ×

File  Edit  View  Insert  Format  Tools  Compose  Help

Send  🖫 🎒  ✂ 🖺 🖺 📎  🕲 🗐  ▼  ! ↓  🗐 🗟

Arial        ▼ 10 ▼  🕲  B I U  📰 📰 📰 📰 📖 🖃 🖅

Message | Options |

To...   | Microsoft                                            |
Cc...   |                                                      |
Subject:| RE: Welcome to Microsoft Outlook!                    |

-----Original Message-----
From:        Microsoft
Sent:        Tuesday, September 17, 1996 3:49 AM
To:          All Users
Subject:     Welcome to Microsoft Outlook!
                 Welcome to Microsoft Outlook
          One Window to Your World of Information

Microsoft Outlook is a desktop information management application that lets you organize
your e-mail, plan your schedule, manage your tasks and contacts, view and open your files
```

2. Type your response. Outlook automatically displays the contents of the original message below your response. You can delete as much of the original message as you want by selecting the text and pressing the Delete key.

3. Click the Send button.

Sending e-mail

To send a new e-mail message, follow these steps:

1. Click the New Mail button to make the dialog box shown in the following figure appear:

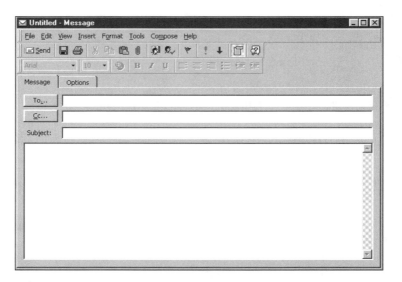

2. In the To... text box, type the e-mail address of the recipient (or recipients). If you want to pick names from your contacts list, click the To... button. A dialog box listing all your contacts who have e-mail addresses appears; select the recipient you want and then click the OK button.

3. Type the e-mail address of anyone you want to receive a courtesy copy of the message in the Cc field. To pick names from your address book, click the Cc button.

4. Type the subject of your message in the Subject text box.

5. Type the body of your message in the message area, the large text box at the bottom of the Message dialog box.

6. Click the Send button in the toolbar.

To attach a file to your message, click the Attach button to bring up an Attach dialog box. Select the file you want to attach from this dialog box and then click the OK button.

Tasks

Outlook enables you to keep a task list, which is a constant reminder that you have miles to go before you sleep. . . and miles to go before you sleep. To work with tasks, click the Task icon or choose Go⇨Tasks. The following figure shows the Outlook task list:

Creating a task

To add an item to your task list, follow these steps:

1. Click the Task icon and then click `Click here to add a new task`.

2. Type a description for the thing you need to do.

3. Press Enter. Outlook adds the task to the top of the Task List.

4. To specify additional information about the task, double-click the task in the Task List. The Task dialog box appears, as shown in the following figure:

5. Type any relevant information such as the due date or status in the Task dialog box. For example, specify a due date by clicking the Due radio button and selecting a due date from the drop-down due date field.

6. Click the Save and Close button after you finish creating your task.

Sigh. You have so much to do.

Part VIII

The Microsoft Office 97 Applets

Most people buy Microsoft Office 97 to get the big programs: Word 97, Excel 97, PowerPoint 97, Access 97, and Outlook. However, Office 97 comes with a respectable collection of smaller programs, called *applets*, which can be used along with the main Office 97 programs. This part shows how these applet programs work.

In this part . . .

- ✔ **Inserting clip art, pictures, sound, and video by using Microsoft Clip Gallery**

- ✔ **Creating Einsteinian equations by using Microsoft Equation Editor**

- ✔ **Creating spectacular charts by using Microsoft Graph**

- ✔ **Compiling organization charts by using Microsoft Organization Chart**

- ✔ **Making fancy text images by using Microsoft WordArt**

Microsoft Clip Gallery

Microsoft Clip Gallery is a nifty little program that enables you to easily insert clip art, pictures, sounds, and videos in your documents. Clip Gallery organizes your pictures, sounds, and videos into categories, such as Architecture, Flags, and Gestures.

To insert a Clip Gallery object in Word 97, PowerPoint 97, or Excel 97, follow these steps:

1. Position the insertion point at the location in your file where you want to insert the clip art, picture, sound, or video clip.

2. Choose Insert➪Picture➪Clip Art from the menu bar.

   The Clip Gallery dialog box appears, as shown in the following figure:

   Note: To insert a picture, sound or video, click the Pictures, Sounds or Video tab.

3. Select from the category list the category that contains the object you want and then select from the box of examples the object that you want to copy into your document.

4. Click the Insert button.

   Clip Gallery inserts the object into your document, as shown in the following figure:

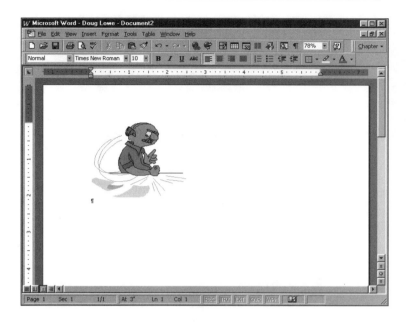

Microsoft Equation Editor

Microsoft Equation Editor is a special version of a NASA-style
equation editor program called MathType, which was created by
Design Science. The applet is designed for use with Word 97 or
PowerPoint 97, but you can use Equation Editor with Excel 97 and
Access 97 as well (assuming, of course, that you can find a reason for
adding a diagram of a complex math equation to an Excel 97 or
Access 97 file, which seems unlikely).

Inserting an equation

The following procedure works with Word 97, Excel 97, or
PowerPoint 97:

   1. Position the insertion point at the location in your file where you
   want to insert the equation.

   2. Choose Insert⇨Object. The Object dialog box appears, as shown
   in the following figure:

3. Select Microsoft Equation 3.0 from the Object Type list box and then click the OK button. Equation Editor takes over, displaying its own menu bar and a floating toolbar of buttons that you use to create the equation.

4. Start typing your equation.

To add a symbol that's not on the keyboard, click the appropriate button in the top row of the Equation Editor toolbar. This reveals a menu of symbols; click the one you want to use.

To add a stacked symbol, click the appropriate button in the bottom row of the toolbar. This pops up a menu of stacked symbols called *templates*. Click the template you want, and the template is inserted into the equation.

(The following section, "Equation Editor buttons," summarizes the functions of all these buttons.)

5. After you create your equation, click anywhere outside the equation. Equation Editor leaves gracefully, returning you to your original program.

Equation Editor buttons

The following table summarizes the buttons in the top row of the Equation Editor toolbar, which you use to insert symbols into an equation:

Button	Symbols It Inserts
≤≠≈	Greater-than and less-than signs and similar symbols
∆ a͟b ∴	Spaces in various sizes plus a few random dots
x̌ a̋ ∷	Cool top hats and things of that sort

Button	Symbols It Inserts
± • ⊗	A collection of operators that aren't found on the keyboard (+ and − are)
→ ⇔ ↓	Various and sundry arrows
∴ ∀ ∃	Logical operators
∉ ∩ ⊂	Symbols for set theory
∂ ∞ ℓ	Miscellaneous symbols (as if they aren't all miscellaneous!)
λ ω θ	Greek letters
Λ Ω ⊛	More Greek letters

The following table summarizes the buttons found in the bottom row of the Equation Editor toolbar, which you use to insert templates into an equation. (A *template,* in this applet, is simply a predefined layout for equation elements, which you can use to create fractions, radicals, and other types of equations.)

Button	Templates It Inserts
(▯) [▯]	Big parentheses, brackets, braces, and the like
▦ √▯	Templates for creating fractions and roots (like, radical, man)
▓ ▯	Templates with little boxes above or below for superscripts or subscripts
Σ▯ Σ▯	Summation templates for using that big Greek Fraternity Sigma thing
∫▯ ∮▯	Integral templates (I knew that I should have paid more attention in calculus class.)
▔▯ ▯▁	Templates with bars above or below the equation
→▯ ←▯	Arrows with templates for text above or below the arrow
▯̇ ∪̇	Templates for working with sets
▯▯▯ ▦	Matrices of templates

Microsoft Graph

Microsoft Graph is a charting program that can create pie charts, bar charts, line charts, and just about every other type of chart imaginable. Graph is intended for use in Word 97, PowerPoint 97, or Access 97. (A charting feature similar to Graph, the Chart Wizard, is built into Excel 97. Look in Part IV of this book for a detailed procedure for using the Excel Chart Wizard.)

To create a chart in Word 97, PowerPoint 97, or Access 97, follow these steps:

1. Place the insertion point at the location in your document where you want the chart to appear.

2. Use one of the following methods to insert a chart, depending on the program you're using:

- **Word 97:** Click the Insert Chart button or choose Insert➪Picture➪Chart from the menu bar.

- **PowerPoint 97:** Click the Insert Chart button or choose Insert➪Chart from the menu bar.

- **Access 97:** Choose Insert➪Chart from the menu bar.

Whichever method you use, Microsoft Graph comes to life. The applet displays its own menus and toolbars plus a chart and datasheet, using sample data to get you started, as shown in the following figure:

3. Type your own data in the datasheet to replace the sample data that Graph provides. To type the data in a cell, click the cell and type the data. You can also use the Tab key to move from cell to cell.

4. Click anywhere outside the chart to return to the program from which you accessed Graph.

The chart remains in the document, and the Word 97, Access 97, or PowerPoint 97 regular menus and toolbars return to view.

Microsoft Organization Chart

Microsoft Organization Chart is a slick little program that creates organization charts, such as those that document corporate structure or federal bureaucracy. The applet is designed for use with PowerPoint 97, but you can use the applet from any Office 97 program that has an Insert⇨Object command on its menu bar.

Adding boxes

To add a new box to an organization chart, follow these steps:

1. Click the appropriate box button in the toolbar for the type of box you want to add.

Note: The table following these steps summarizes the functions of those buttons.

2. Click the existing box to which you want the new box to be attached. The box is added to the chart.

3. Type the name and, if you want, a title and comments in the new box.

Button	What It Does
Subordinate:	Inserts a new box subordinate to the box you click
:Co-worker	Inserts a Co-worker box to the left of the box you click
Co-worker:	Inserts a Co-worker box to the right of the box you click
Manager:	Inserts a Manager box above the box you click
Assistant:	Inserts an Assistant box beside the box you click

Creating an organization chart

Follow these steps to create an organization chart:

1. Position the insertion point at the location in your file where you want to insert the organization chart.

2. In PowerPoint 97, choose Insert⇨Picture⇨Organization Chart from the menu bar; in other programs, choose Insert⇨Object to summon the Insert Object dialog box. Then select MS Organization Chart 2.0 and click the OK button.

Either way, Organization Chart appears in its own window, as shown in the following figure:

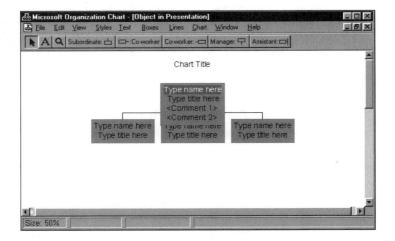

3. Click each box in the organization chart and then type a new name, title, and any other information you want to appear in the chart.

4. To add a new box to the chart, click the appropriate button in the toolbar, click the box to which you want the new box attached, and then type a new name, title, and other information for the box.

(For more information about adding boxes, see the preceding section, "Adding boxes.")

The following figure shows what a finished organization chart looks like:

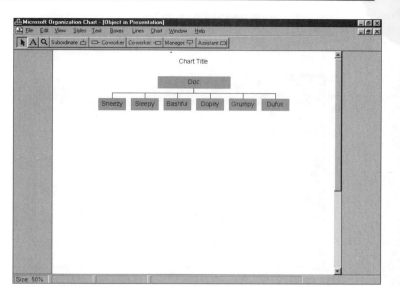

5. Choose File⇨Exit and Return from the Organization Chart menu bar to return to your program.

6. After the applet asks if you want to update the object in your document, click the Yes button.

You return to your original document with the organization chart in place.

Microsoft WordArt

Microsoft WordArt is specially designed for formatting text in strange ways. You usually use the applet to create logos. Although the name suggests that WordArt is intended for use with Word 97, the applet works just as well with PowerPoint 97 and Excel 97. (You can also use WordArt in Access 97 via the Insert⇨Object command, but that procedure isn't covered here.)

The following procedure works with Word 97, Excel 97, and PowerPoint 97:

1. Position the insertion point at the location in your file where you want to insert the WordArt object.

In Word 97 or PowerPoint 97, just click the mouse pointer to mark the location. In Excel 97, highlight the range of cells into which you want to insert the WordArt object.

2. Choose Insert⇨Picture⇨WordArt.

The WordArt Gallery appears, as shown in the following figure:

3. Select the WordArt style you'd like and then click the OK button. The Edit WordArt Text dialog box appears, as shown in the following figure:

4. Type the text you want to use in the Text box, and if you want, use the Font drop-down list to change the font.

5. Click the OK button. WordArt creates the object in your document, and the WordArt toolbar appears, as shown in the following figure:

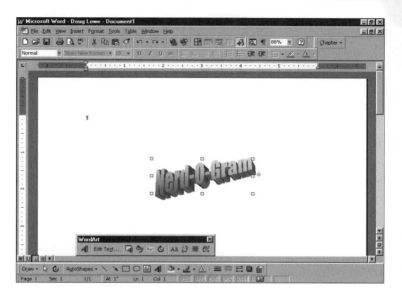

6. Fool around with the controls on the toolbar if you want.

The function of each button is described in the following table:

Button	What It Does
	Creates another WordArt object
Edit Text...	Opens the Edit WordArt Text dialog box so that you can change the text
	Opens the WordArt Gallery so that you can quickly apply a different format
Abc	Enables you to change the shape of the WordArt text
	Enables you to change the rotation angle of the WordArt object
Aa	Alternates between normal letters and same-height letters, in which upper- and lowercase letters are the same height
Ab b↲	Alternates between horizontal and vertical text
	Changes the alignment
AV	Changes the space between letters

7. Click anywhere outside the WordArt object frame to return to the program from which you opened WordArt.

The WordArt object remains in the document and the Word 97, Excel 97, or PowerPoint 97 regular menus and toolbars return to view.

Part IX

Working Together

It never fails. You finally finish that pesky projected income worksheet you've been working on for days when your boss asks you to give a ten-minute presentation about it at tomorrow's stockholders' meeting and deliver a ten-page written report on income trends by the end of the week. Wouldn't it be great if you could incorporate the Excel 97 worksheet into a PowerPoint 97 presentation and then convert the entire presentation into a Word 97 document?

As luck has it, you can do just that. In fact, you can do several things to accomplish this type of sharing. This part describes various techniques and procedures that let you use the programs that come with Microsoft Office 97 together.

Using programs together sometimes goes under the $2 buzzword *integration,* and if this weren't a *...For Dummies* book, this part would probably be titled "Integration" instead of "Working Together." Count your blessings that you're reading a *...For Dummies* book!

In this part . . .

- ✔ Copying and pasting information between Office 97 applications
- ✔ Using OLE to share information
- ✔ Exchanging information between Office 97 applications by using specific features
- ✔ Using Microsoft Binder to create compound documents

The Clipboard

In many cases, the easiest way to share data between Office 97 programs is to use the good ol' Cut-or-Copy-and-Paste-to-the-Clipboard technique that has been a standard part of all Windows programs since the first version of Windows. The following sections describe how to copy and move data by using the Clipboard:

Copying data

To copy data from one program to another, follow these steps:

1. Switch to the program that contains the data you want to copy. If the program isn't already running, start it by choosing it from the Start⇨Programs menu. If the file that contains the data isn't already open, open it.

2. Highlight the data that you want to copy by using the mouse or keyboard.

3. Press Ctrl+C, choose Edit⇨Copy, or click the Copy button, which appears on the Standard toolbar of all the Office 97 programs.

4. Switch to the program into which you want to copy the data. If the program isn't already running, start it by picking it from the Start⇨Programs menu. If the file into which you want the data copied isn't already open, open it.

5. Position the insertion point where you want to insert the data.

6. Press Ctrl+V, choose the Edit⇨Paste, or click the Paste button, which appears on the Standard toolbar of all the Office 97 programs.

Moving data

To move data from one program to another, follow these steps:

1. Switch to the program that contains the data that you want to move. If the program isn't already running, start it by choosing it from the Start⇨Programs menu. If the file that contains the data isn't already open, open it.

2. Highlight the data that you want to move by using the mouse or keyboard.

3. Press Ctrl+X, choose Edit⇨Cut, or click the Cut button, which appears on the Standard toolbar of all the Office 97 programs.

4. Switch to the program into which you want to move the data. If the program isn't already running, start it by choosing it from the Start⇨Programs menu. If the file into which you want the data copied isn't already open, open it.

5. Position the insertion point where you want to insert the data.

 6. Press Ctrl+V, choose Edit⇨Paste, or click the Paste button, which appears on the Standard toolbar of all the Office 97 programs.

Combining Documents with Microsoft Binder

Binder is a nifty program that lets you create special documents that are made up of other types of Office 97 documents. For example, if you are preparing a proposal that includes a Word 97 document, some Excel 97 spreadsheets, and handouts from an Excel 97 presentation, you can bundle all of these documents together in a single Binder document.

To create a new binder, follow these steps:

1. Start Binder by choosing it from the Start⇨Programs menu. A blank binder appears, as shown in the following figure:

```
Microsoft Office Binder - Binder1                    _ □ ×
    ◀▶  File  Go  Section  Help




0 section(s)          0 section(s) selected
```

2. To add an existing file to the binder, choose Section⇨Add from File. Select the file you want to add and then click the Add button. The file is added to the binder and represented as an icon, as shown in the figure that follows:

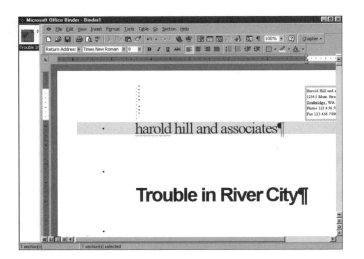

3. To add an empty Office 97 file to a binder, choose Section➪Add. Binder displays all of the available Office 97 templates. Select the template you want by clicking it and then click the OK button. A file based on the template you select is added to the binder. (The template you select determines whether Binder creates a Word 97, Excel 97, or PowerPoint 97 document.)

4. Repeat Steps 2 and 3 for as many files as you want to add to the binder. The following figure shows how a binder appears after several files have been added; as you can see, icons for the files appear at the left edge of the Binder window.

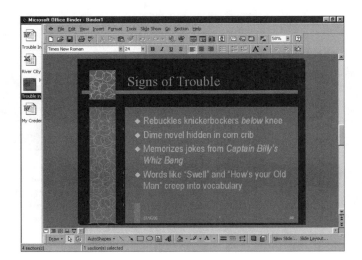

5. Choose File⇨Save Binder to save the binder. Type a name for the binder and then click the Save button.

Linking

Copying data from one program to another is easy enough, but what happens if you need to change the data? If you simply copy the data, you must track down every file to which you copied the data and update the data in each file. But if you *link* the data, any changes that you make to the original version of the data automatically apply to copies of the linked data.

Linking data

To copy data from one program to another and create a link, follow these steps:

1. Switch to the program that contains the data that you want to copy. If the program isn't already running, start it by choosing it from the Start⇨Programs menu. If the file that contains the data isn't already open, open it.

2. Highlight the data that you want to copy by using the mouse or keyboard.

3. Press Ctrl+C, choose Edit⇨Copy, or click the Copy button, which appears on the Standard toolbar of all the Office 97 programs.

4. Switch to the program into which you want to copy the data. If the program isn't already running, start it by choosing it from the Start⇨Programs menu. If the file into which you want the data copied isn't already open, open it.

5. Position the insertion point where you want to insert the data.

6. Choose Edit⇨Paste Special to summon the Paste Special dialog box, shown in this figure:

Paste Special		? X
Source:	Microsoft Excel 8.0 Worksheet Sheet1!R1C1:R5C5	
	As:	OK
⦿ Paste:	Microsoft Excel 8.0 Worksheet Object	Cancel
○ Paste link:	Formatted Text (RTF)	
	Unformatted Text	
	Picture	
	Bitmap	☐ Float over text
	Picture (Enhanced Metafile)	☐ Display as icon
Result	Inserts the contents of the Clipboard as text with font and table formatting.	

7. Click the Paste link radio button.

8. Click the OK button.

Whenever you open the file that contains the link, the program checks to see whether the data has changed. If so, it updates the link. That way, the data that appears in the document will always reflect the most current version of the linked-to document.

Breaking a link

If you grow tired of the link and want to break it, follow this procedure:

1. Open the program and file that contain the link.

2. Choose Edit⇨Links. The Links dialog box appears.

3. Select the link that you want to break from the Source file list.

4. Click the Break Link button.

5. When asked whether you really want to break the link, click the Yes button.

6. If links still remain in the document, you need to click the OK button to dismiss the Links dialog box. If you break the last link, the Links dialog box automatically vanishes.

OLE!

Object Linking and Embedding, or OLE for short, is another way to share information between Office 97 programs. When you use OLE, data is *embedded* into your document as an *object*. When you double-click an embedded object, you summon the program that originally created the object so that you can edit the object.

OLE comes in two flavors, both used by Office 97:

+ **OLE 1:** With OLE 1, a separate window opens when you edit an embedded object.

+ **OLE 2:** You edit the embedded object within the same window as the rest of the document. The program that "owns" the object momentarily takes over the window, supplying its own menus, buttons, and status bar.

Note that you don't get to choose whether you use OLE 1 or OLE 2. That decision is made by the programmers who create the programs you use. Most newer programs use OLE 2, because it provides a slicker way of sharing information between two programs. OLE 1 is used mostly by older programs.

Pasting an OLE object

To paste an OLE object via the Clipboard, follow these steps:

1. Switch to the program that contains the data that you want to embed as an object. If the program isn't already running, start it by choosing it from the Start⇨Programs menu on the Windows 95 taskbar. If the file that contains the data isn't already open, open it.

2. Highlight the data that you want to embed by using the mouse or keyboard.

3. Press Ctrl+C, choose Edit⇨Copy, or click the Copy button, which appears on the Standard toolbar of all the Office 97 programs.

4. Switch to the program into which you want to embed the object. If the program isn't already running, start it by choosing it from the Start⇨Programs menu. If the file into which you want the data copied isn't already open, open it.

5. Position the insertion point where you want the embedded object to appear.

6. Choose Edit⇨Paste Special to summon the Paste Special dialog box.

Paste Special ? ☒

Source: Microsoft Excel 8.0 Worksheet
Sheet1!R1C1:R5C5

As:

☐ Paste:
☑ Paste link:

Microsoft Excel 8.0 Worksheet Object
Formatted Text (RTF)
Unformatted Text
Picture
Bitmap
Word Hyperlink

OK
Cancel

☑ Float over text
☐ Display as icon

Result

Inserts the contents of the Clipboard as a picture.

Paste Link creates a shortcut to the source file.
Changes to the source file will be reflected in your
document.

7. Click the Paste link radio button. The Paste Special dialog box lists the various forms in which you can paste the contents of the Clipboard.

8. Pick the one that indicates the data that should be pasted as an object. For example, to embed Excel 97 spreadsheet data as an object, choose Microsoft Excel 8.0 Worksheet Object.

9. Click the OK button. The data is inserted as an object.

TIP

You can also use a drag-and-drop technique to paste an OLE object. Start by arranging your windows so that the data you want to copy and the program in which you want to embed the object are both visible. Next, select the data you want to copy. Then hold down the Ctrl key and drag the data over to the document in which you want to embed the object. When you release the mouse button, the data you selected is inserted as an object.

Simple text copied in this way is pasted as text rather than inserted as an object. An object is inserted whenever you attempt to copy data that cannot be directly edited by the program to which you copy the data — for example, if you copy a range of Excel 97 worksheet cells to a Word 97 document.

Creating a new OLE object

To create a new OLE object, follow this procedure:

1. In the program and file into which you want to embed the object, position the insertion point where you want the embedded object to appear.

2. Choose Insert⬧Object to summon the Object dialog box, as shown in the following figure:

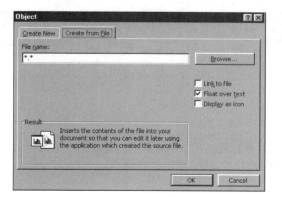

3. Make sure that the Create New tab is selected. If it isn't, click it.

4. The Object type box lists the various types of objects that you can create. Pick the type of object you want. For example, to create an Equation object, choose Microsoft Equation 3.0.

5. Click the OK button to insert the object. The program that creates the object type you selected runs so that you can edit the new object.

Inserting a file as an OLE object

To insert an existing file as an embedded OLE object, follow these steps:

1. In the program and file into which you want to insert the existing file, position the insertion point where you want the embedded object to appear.

2. Choose Insert➪Object to summon the Object dialog box.

3. Click the Create from File tab. The Object dialog box appears as shown in the following figure:

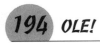

4. Click the <u>B</u>rowse button. Doing so brings up a Browse dialog box, which is similar to the familiar Open dialog box.

5. Select the file you want to embed from the list of files that appears in the Browse dialog box. You may have to rummage about the disk a bit to locate the file.

6. Click the OK button to return to the Object dialog box and then click the OK button again. The file is inserted as an object.

Editing an OLE object

To edit an embedded OLE object, simply double-click the object in the document. For example, if you use Microsoft Organization Chart to create an organization chart in a Word 97 document, you can change the chart by double-clicking on the organization chart. This fires up Microsoft Organization Chart so you can edit your chart.

When you edit an OLE 1 object, the program that created the object is called forward and appears in its own window, as shown in the following figure:

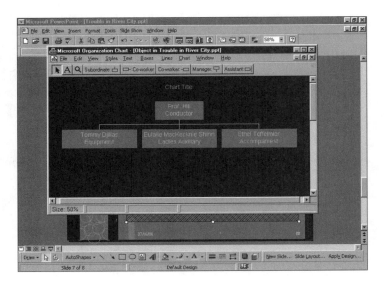

You can create a hyperlink in Word 97, Excel 97, PowerPoint 97, or Access 97 by choosing <u>I</u>nsert⇨<u>H</u>yper<u>l</u>ink. This summons an Insert Hyperlink dialog box in which you can specify the location you would like the Hyperlink to lead to. Type the filename in this field and click the OK button to create the hyperlink.

You can edit the object any way you want. After you finish editing the object, choose File⇨Exit and Return.

When you edit an OLE 2 object, the program that created the object takes over the program in which the object is embedded, replacing the original program's menus and toolbars with its own as shown in the following figure:

After you finish editing the object, click anywhere outside the object's boundaries.

Deleting an OLE object

To delete an embedded object, click it to select it and then press Delete.

Using Hyperlinks

Hyperlinks are "hot spots" in an Office 97 document that, when clicked, jump to a specific location within the current document, open another Office 97 document, or display a page from the World Wide Web. By creating hyperlinks to other Office 97 documents, you can effectively share information among documents without going to the trouble of using OLE or the Paste Link command. For example, a Word 97 document that contains a marketing proposal may include a hyperlink to an Excel 97 chart that shows a sales chart.

When you come across a hyperlink in a document, you can jump to the document that the hyperlink refers to by simply clicking the hyperlink. When you do, the Web toolbar appears, providing several buttons you can click to move back and forth among hyperlinked documents, just as you do when exploring the World Wide Web using a Web browser such as Internet Explorer. The two buttons you use most on this toolbar are

+ **Back:** This button returns you to the document that led to the current document.

+ **Forward:** After you use the Back button to go to a previously viewed document, you can retrace your steps forward again by clicking this button.

Sharing Information between Word 97 and Excel 97

Office 97 includes several features that are specifically designed to allow you to exchange information between Word 97 and Excel 97.

Exchanging tables between Word 97 and Excel 97

When you copy or cut a range of cells from an Excel 97 worksheet and paste it into a Word 97 document, the worksheet data automatically converts to a Word 97 table. If the Excel 97 worksheet includes formulas, the formulas' calculated values are pasted into Word 97.

Likewise, when you copy or cut a Word 97 table to the Clipboard and then paste it into an Excel 97 worksheet, the table data automatically converts to worksheet cells.

Inserting an Excel 97 worksheet in a Word 97 document

To insert an empty Excel 97 worksheet object into a Word 97 document, follow the procedure described under "Inserting a file as an OLE object," previously in this part. In the Object dialog box, specify Microsoft Excel Worksheet as the object type.

 You can also use the Insert Microsoft Excel Microsoft Worksheet button from the Standard toolbar. When you click this button, a grid-like menu appears, allowing you to indicate the size of the worksheet you want to insert into your document.

Using Excel 97 data in a mail merge

Office 97 provides four places to store the names and addresses from the Word 97 mail merge feature: a Word 97 table, an Excel 97 worksheet, an Access 97 table, and the Outlook contacts list. To use an Excel 97 worksheet as a mail merge data source, follow these steps:

1. In Excel 97, create a worksheet that contains the names and addresses to which you want to mail. The database should be kept in a range of cells with one row for each record and one column for each field, such as Name, Address, City, State, Zip Code. Here's an example of an Excel 97 worksheet:

2. Save the file, exit Excel 97, and switch to Word 97.

3. Choose Tools⇨Mail Merge. The Mail Merge Helper dialog box appears.

4. Click the Create button to create the main document. Choose Form Letters and then select New Main Document to type a new letter.

5. Click the Get Data button and then select the Open Data Source option.

6. When the Open Data Source dialog box appears, select MS Excel Worksheets (*.xls) for the file type, as shown in the figure that follows:

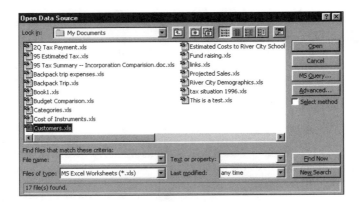

7. Find your file and then click the Open button. Word 97 asks whether you want to include the entire spreadsheet or just a range of cells.

8. Click the OK button to include the entire worksheet. Mail Merge informs you that your main document doesn't contain any merge fields:

> Word found no merge fields in your main document. Choose the Edit Main Document button to insert merge fields into your main document.
>
> Edit Main Document   Cancel

9. Click the Edit Main Document button. You go to the main document window with the Mail Merge toolbar visible. Type your letter, clicking the Insert Merge Field button whenever you want a merge field to appear.

10. To merge your letters, choose Tools⇨Mail Merge to summon the Mail Merge Helper dialog box. Click the Merge button to bring up the Merge dialog box. Finally, click the Merge button to merge the letters. Word 97 creates a new document to hold the merged letters.

Sharing Information between Word 97 and PowerPoint 97

Other than copying text and graphics via the Clipboard, several specific Office 97 features are designed to share data between Word 97 and PowerPoint 97. These features are covered in the following sections:

Using Write-Up

PowerPoint 97 includes a new feature called Write-Up that lets you convert a presentation to Word 97 format. Here's how to use the new Write-Up feature:

1. In PowerPoint 97, open the presentation that you want to convert.

2. Choose File➪Send To➪Microsoft Word. The Write-Up dialog box appears, as shown in the following figure:

3. Write-Up provides several options for how you want to format the presentation in Word 97, as indicated by the sample document styles shown next to the radio buttons. Choose the formatting option you want by clicking its radio button.

The Paste and Paste Link options determine whether a link should be established between the original PowerPoint 97 presentation and the converted Word 97 document. If you select the Paste option, no link is established. If you specify Paste Lir' a link is created so that whenever the slides in the original PowerPoint 97 presentation change, the corresponding s' the converted Word 97 document change as well.

4. Click the OK button and then wait while Write-Up launches Word 97 and converts your presentation. This may take a few moments, but eventually the presentation will appear in Word 97 as an open document.

5. Choose File⇨Save if you want to save the converted file.

Inserting a Word 97 outline in PowerPoint 97

You can convert a Word 97 document to a PowerPoint 97 presentation provided that the Word 97 document uses standard heading styles such as Heading 1 and Heading 2 to indicate its outline. Here's the procedure:

1. In PowerPoint 97, create a new presentation or open an existing presentation into which you want the Word 97 outline inserted. Place the insertion point where you want to insert the outline in the presentation. (This is best done in Outline view.)

2. Choose Insert⇨Slides from Outline. The Insert Outline dialog box appears:

3. Pick the file that contains the outline you want to convert and then click the Insert button.

4. Wait. If the document is big, this process can take a few minutes. When PowerPoint 97 finishes chomping on the outline, the outline appears as part of the current presentation.

TIP

Another way to convert a Word 97 document to a PowerPoint 97 presentation is to open the document in Word 97 and then choose File⇨Send To⇨Microsoft PowerPoint.

Creating a Word 97 table in a PowerPoint 97 presentation

Word 97 has a powerful Table feature that lets you create perfectly formatted tables. PowerPoint 97 has no such feature, but it does have the ability to let you create a Word 97 table right inside a PowerPoint 97 document. Thus, all of the Word table-handling features are available to you whenever you work in PowerPoint 97. To insert an empty Word 97 table into a PowerPoint 97 presentation, follow this procedure:

1. In PowerPoint 97, move to the slide where you want to insert the table.

 2. Click the Insert Microsoft Word Table button on the Standard toolbar.

3. Hold down the mouse button and drag to indicate the size of the table that you want to insert, as shown in this figure:

4. Release the mouse button. The table is inserted into PowerPoint 97, with the Word 97 menus and toolbars present for editing the table as shown in the following figure:

5. Edit the table any way you want, inserting any values and applying any formats.

6. After you finish editing the table, click anywhere outside the table. PowerPoint 97 returns to its normal appearance.

To edit the table later, just double-click it.

Sharing Information between PowerPoint 97 and Excel 97

PowerPoint 97 allows you to insert an Excel 97 chart or worksheet into a presentation. You can also create a graph in PowerPoint 97 that is linked to worksheet data in an Excel 97 worksheet.

Linking a PowerPoint 97 graph to Excel 97 data

To create a graph in PowerPoint 97 that is linked to data in an Excel 97 worksheet, follow these steps:

1. Create the worksheet in Excel 97 and save the file. Then select the cells that contain the data you want to graph and press Ctrl+C to copy those cells to the Clipboard.

2. In PowerPoint 97, click the Insert Chart button to create a graph. A sample graph and its data sheet appear, as shown in the following figure:

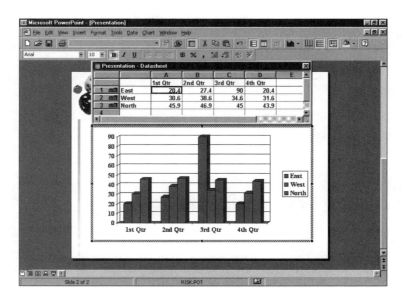

3. Select the entire range of sample data in the data sheet and then press the Delete key to delete it.

4. Choose Edit⇨Paste Link.

5. When PowerPoint 97 warns that you are about to replace existing data in the datasheet, click the OK button. The data is pasted into the data sheet and the chart adjusted as necessary.

6. Change whatever chart settings you wish. For example, the following figure shows how the chart appears after I paste the data, choose a pie chart for the chart type, and change the Data in Columns setting to Data in Rows:

7. Click anywhere outside the chart to return PowerPoint 97 to its normal display.

Because the chart is based on data that is linked to data in the Excel 97 worksheet, the chart is automatically updated whenever data in the worksheet is changed.

Sharing Information between Word 97 and Access 97

The most useful way to work with Access 97 data from Word 97 is to use Access 97 as the data source for a mail merge. You can also insert Access 97 data into a Word 97 table.

Using Access 97 data in a mail merge

You have two ways to use Access 97 data in a mail merge. The first, described in this section, is to summon the Word 97 Mail Merge Helper to use an Access 97 database as the mail merge data source. The second, described later in this part, is to use the Access 97 Mail Merge Wizard to export Access 97 data to Word 97.

Both procedures get the job done; your choice depends on whether you're more familiar with Word 97 or Access 97. If you're at home with Word 97, use this procedure. If you're more familiar with Access 97, follow the steps under the heading "Merge It With MSWord" later in this part.

Here's the procedure for using Access 97 data in a Word 97 mail merge:

1. In Access 97, create a database that contains names and addresses. Use whatever field names you want: First Name, Last Name, Address, City, State, and Zip Code seem likely candidates.

2. Save the file, exit Access 97, and switch to Word 97.

3. Choose Tools⇨Mail Merge. The Mail Merge Helper dialog box appears.

4. Click the Create button to create the main document. Pick Form Letters and then select New Main Document to type a new letter.

5. Click the Get Data button and then select the Open Data Source option. When the Open Data Source dialog box appears, select MS Access Databases (*.mdb) as the file type, as shown in the following figure:

6. Select the file you want to use and then click the Open button. The following dialog box appears:

```
Microsoft Access                    [?][X]

 Tables | Queries |

 Tables in Northwind.mdb:
 ┌──────────────────────────────────┐
 │ Categories                       ▲│
 │ Customers                         │
 │ Employees                         │
 │ Order Details                     │
 │ Orders                            │
 │ Products                          │
 │ Shippers                          │
 │ Suppliers                        ▼│
 └──────────────────────────────────┘

  ┌────────┐  ┌────────┐  ┌──────────┐
  │   OK   │  │ Cancel │  │ View SQL...│
  └────────┘  └────────┘  └──────────┘
```

7. Pick the table or query you want and then click the OK button. Mail Merge informs you that your main document doesn't contain any merge fields.

8. Click Edit Main Document. You are taken to the main document window with the Mail Merge toolbar visible. Type your letter, clicking the Insert Merge Field button wherever you want a merge field to appear.

9. To merge your letters, choose Tools⇨Mail Merge to bring forth the Mail Merge Helper dialog box. Click the Merge button to bring up the Merge dialog box. Finally, click the Merge button to merge the letters. Word 97 creates a new document to hold the merge letters.

Inserting Access 97 data into a Word 97 table

To copy data from an Access 97 database to a Word 97 table, follow these steps:

1. In Word 97, summon the Database toolbar by choosing View⇨Toolbars⇨Database. The Database toolbar appears, usually immediately beneath the Formatting toolbar (but it may appear in a different location if you or someone else has previously moved it).

2. Click the Insert Database button. The Database dialog box appears, as shown in the figure that follows:

3. Click the Get Data button.

4. When the Open Data Source dialog box appears, select MS Access Databases (*.mdb) as the file type, as shown.

5. Select the database file that contains the data you want to use and then click the Open button. The following dialog box appears:

6. Pick the table you want and then click the OK button. You return to the Database dialog box.

7. Click Insert Data. The Insert Data dialog box appears, as shown in the following figure:

8. Click the OK button. The data is inserted into a table, as shown here:

You may notice that the table columns are too narrow to accommodate the data that's stored. The table looks like it's jumbled up, but the data is actually stored in the table correctly. If you want, you can adjust the column widths to give the table a neater appearance.

Sharing Access 97 Data with Excel 97 and Word 97

Access 97 offers several features specially designed to share data with other Office 97 applications. The following sections describe some of these features.

Merge It With MSWord

The Merge It With MSWord command provides an easy way to use Access 97 data in a Word 97 mail merge. Just follow these steps:

1. In Access 97, open the database that contains the table that you want to use in a mail merge.

2. Select the table or query that you want to convert to the mail merge data source.

3. Choose Tools⇨Office Links⇨Merge It With MSWord. The Microsoft Word Mail Merge Wizard dialog box appears.

4. If the letter that you want to use for the mail merge already exists, click the Link your data to an existing Microsoft Word document, click the OK button, select the document, and then click the OK button again. If you haven't yet created the document, click the Create a new document and then link the data to its radio button and then click the OK button.

5. Watch as Access 97 launches Word 97 and exports database data into the mail merge data source ready to be merged with the main document.

Publish It With MSWord

You can convert an Access 97 table, query, form, or report to a Word 97 table by using the Publish It With MSWord command. Here is the procedure:

1. In Access 97, open the database that contains the database object that you want to convert to a Word 97 document.

2. Select the database object (a table, query, form, or report) that you want to convert.

3. Choose Tools➪OfficeLinks➪Publish It With MSWord.

4. Watch as Access 97 converts the data to a Word 97 document.

Converting Access 97 data to Excel 97

You can easily convert an Access 97 database table, query, or report to an Excel 97 worksheet by following this procedure:

1. In Access 97, open the database that contains the database object that you want to convert to Excel 97.

2. Select the table, query, or report that you want to convert.

3. Choose Tools➪OfficeLinks➪Analyze It With MS Excel.

4. Watch as Access 97 converts the data to an Excel 97 worksheet and then launches Excel 97 and opens the newly created file.

Index

A

ABS function (Excel 97), 88
Access 97, 11
  adding fields to existing tables,
    130–132
  converting Access 97 data to
    Excel 97, 208
  creating a new database, 132–136
  creating queries, 136–140
  creating reports, 140–145
  as a data source for a mail merge,
    203–205
  entering and editing data,
    145–147
  Form Wizard, 151–155
  inserting Access data into Word
    table, 205–207
  Publish to the Web Wizard,
    147–151
Access 97 For Windows 95 For
  Dummies, 129
address (Excel 97), 102
address book (Outlook), 165–167
Alt key combinations
  Alt+Esc for next program, 31
  Alt+F4 for Exit command, 23
  Alt+F4 to exit programs, 17
  Alt+Tab for toggling all open
    programs, 31
animation in PowerPoint 97,
  108–110
annotating cells (Excel 97), 84–85
applets, 12–14
  Clip Gallery, 13, 174–175
  Equation Editor, 13, 175–177

Graph, 13, 178–179
  Organization Chart, 14, 179–181
  WordArt, 14, 181–184
appointments, scheduling
  (Outlook), 158–165
  events, 160–161
  meetings, 162–163
  recurring appointments,
    163–165
art
  adding art to a PowerPoint 97
    presentation, 110–111
  Clip Gallery applet, 13, 174–175
  WordArt, 181–184
AutoComplete (Word 97), 8
AutoFormatting in Excel 97, 78–79
AVERAGE function (Excel 97), 88

B

background objects, hiding
  (PowerPoint 97), 114–115
background for Web page, 46
Binder
  combining documents of
    various programs, 187–189
  described, 13
boilerplate letter, 53–54
boldface
  keyboard shortcut for, 23
  as used in this book, 5
  in Word 97 documents, 50
bomb (WARNING!) icon, 4
borders around text in Word 97, 34
Browse menu in Word 97, 35–36
bulleted lists (Word 97), 36

C

Notes

Notes

WWW.DUMMIES.COM

Discover Dummies Online!

The Dummies Web Site is your fun and friendly online resource for the latest information about ...For Dummies® books and your favorite topics. The Web site is the place to communicate with us, exchange ideas with other ...For Dummies readers, chat with authors, and have fun!

Ten Fun and Useful Things You Can Do at www.dummies.com

1. Win free ...For Dummies books and more!
2. Register your book and be entered in a prize drawing.
3. Meet your favorite authors through the IDG Books Author Chat Series.
4. Exchange helpful information with other ...For Dummies readers.
5. Discover other great ...For Dummies books you must have!
6. Purchase Dummieswear™ exclusively from our Web site.
7. Buy ...For Dummies books online.
8. Talk to us. Make comments, ask questions, get answers!
9. Download free software.
10. Find additional useful resources from authors.

Link directly to these ten fun and useful things at **http://www.dummies.com/10useful**

For other technology titles from IDG Books Worldwide, go to
www.idgbooks.com

Not on the Web yet? It's easy to get started with *Dummies 101*®: *The Internet For Windows*® *95* or *The Internet For Dummies*®, *4th Edition*, at local retailers everywhere.

Find other ...For Dummies books on these topics:
Business • Career • Databases • Food & Beverage • Games • Gardening • Graphics
Hardware • Health & Fitness • Internet and the World Wide Web • Networking
Office Suites • Operating Systems • Personal Finance • Pets • Programming • Recreation
Sports • Spreadsheets • Teacher Resources • Test Prep • Word Processing

IDG BOOKS WORLDWIDE BOOK REGISTRATION

Register This Book and Win!

We want to hear from you!

Visit **http://my2cents.dummies.com** to register this book and tell us how you liked it!

- ✔ Get entered in our monthly prize giveaway.

- ✔ Give us feedback about this book — tell us what you like best, what you like least, or maybe what you'd like to ask the author and us to change!

- ✔ Let us know any other *...For Dummies* topics that interest you.

Your feedback helps us determine what books to publish, tells us what coverage to add as we revise our books, and lets us know whether we're meeting your needs as a *...For Dummies* reader. You're our most valuable resource, and what you have to say is important to us!

Not on the Web yet? It's easy to get started with *Dummies 101®: The Internet For Windows® 95* or *The Internet For Dummies*, 4th Edition, at local retailers everywhere.

Or let us know what you think by sending us a letter at the following address:

...For Dummies Book Registration
Dummies Press
7260 Shadeland Station, Suite 100
Indianapolis, IN 46256
Fax 317-596-5498

BUSINESS AND
GENERAL
REFERENCE
BOOK SERIES
FROM IDG

COMPUTER
BOOK SERIES
FROM IDG